CÉZANNE

CÉZANNE

by
Constance Naubert-Riser

STUDIO EDITIONS

LONDON

Originally published by Fernand Hazan, Paris 1991

This edition published 1991 by Studio Editions Ltd,
Princess House, 50 Eastcastle Street,
London W1N 7AP, England

ISBN 1-85170-815-4

Printed and bound in Hong Kong

A difficult apprenticeship

In April 1861 Paul Cézanne arrived in Paris; at twenty-two he was full of hope and fiercely determined to become a painter. The path to success was a well-established one: the first step was to register with one of the open studios that prepared students for the entrance examination of the École des Beaux-Arts, an institution that held the monopoly in art education and aesthetic standards. Another important lesson learned in these studios was how to make a first submission to the annual Salon in order to obtain the best chance of success. This was crucial to a young artist, since having a painting accepted by the all-powerful Salon jury gave access to a network of potential buyers, particularly if the work evoked favourable comment from a critic.

The most renowned studios, where students received regular correction of their work, were run by professors from the École des Beaux-Arts. At the start of their careers, Manet, Renoir, Bazille, Monet and Sisley all attended the studios of either Couture or Gleyre, which were the most respected. Cézanne, however, chose to register at the Académie Suisse. Here, for a very small sum, one could work straight away from a live model, without following a detailed pedagogical programme and without having to submit to mandatory marking sessions.

The reasons behind Cézanne's choice of studio are not clear. Was it a decision made through ignorance of the possibilities available to aspiring artists in Paris at that time? Was it simply because, at the suggestion of his friend Zola, he regarded the Académie Suisse as one of the least expensive? Was Cézanne concerned to maintain his independence, or did he lack confidence and hope to improve his technique before appearing in any of the more illustrious studios? Whatever the answer, the route

he opted for proved to be longer and more arduous than he had anticipated. Cézanne's career did not really start until 1872, when he moved to Pontoise and began working regularly in the company of Camille Pissarro, whom he had first encountered eleven years earlier at the Académie Suisse. Prior to this date, his paintings, his sketchbooks and his correspondence with those closest to him all reveal glimpses of difficulties and bouts of discouragement – on both the personal and professional fronts – that must inevitably have delayed the full flowering of his talent.

Cézanne, who was born on 19 January 1839, in Aix-en-Provence, divided his childhood and adolescent years between school and long expeditions into the idyllic countryside surrounding his home town, in the company of classmates Émile Zola and Baptistin Baille. Passionately fond of poetry, the three boys recited Homer and Virgil and developed a keen taste for Victor Hugo and Alfred de Musset. From 1857 on, while he was still at school, the young Cézanne's particular interest in art prompted him to start taking classes at the local municipal drawing school. Then in 1858, somewhat abruptly, Zola went to Paris to join his mother.

The separation of the two young men resulted in a regular correspondence that throws light on some of the obstacles that blocked Cézanne's path. After passing his baccalauréat in November of that year, he registered – much against his will – at the law school in Aix, pressed to do so by his banker father, who was concerned about the future management of his fortune. A letter from Zola to Cézanne (December 1859) is the first reference we have to the latter's intention to devote himself entirely to painting and, more specifically, to the paternal veto to

Self-portrait with Palette, c. 1885.

which he was subject.[1] Encouraged by Zola, already a frequent visitor to the studios of artists whose work he would soon be defending as a critic, Cézanne finally succeeded, in 1861, in obtaining his family's permission to pursue his chosen career in Paris, together with the promise of a monthly allowance.

But, alas, his enthusiasm for the Salon, for the 'magnificent Meissoniers', for a 'staggering' painting by Gustave Doré and for simply being able to witness Gérôme, Glaise, Cabanel and Courbet competing for the 'honour of victory' was not sufficient to assuage the 'anguish' that dogged him. In spite of the long morning hours at the Académie Suisse, the afternoons spent listening to the advice of a fellow native of Aix, the painter Villevielle, and even in spite of the pleasure derived from his visits to the Louvre and Luxembourg, Cézanne became discouraged by his lack of progress and, in September 1861, renounced painting and returned to Aix, where he started work at his father's bank.

His passion for painting did not remain dormant for long, however, and by November 1862 he was back at the Académie Suisse. Upon failing the entrance exam to the École des Beaux-Arts – the examiner's comment was, 'He paints to excess' – Cézanne opted for self-education. Rubens and Delacroix, Titian and Veronese became his masters. The literature of the period provided another source of inspiration, and Balzac, Flaubert and Baudelaire were a constant influence on the development of his

1. The letters Cézanne wrote to Zola between 1859 and 1862 are lost. Cézanne's correspondence has been collected and annotated by John Rewald, who has filled the gaps by presenting the letters written by Zola in reply to those that have disappeared. The references for the quotes taken from the latest edition of this correspondence (Paris: Grasset, 1978) will be given thus: Cézanne, *Correspondance*, followed by the page number – in this case, 64.

Louis-Auguste Cézanne, the Artist's Father, reading "L'Événement", 1866.

The Murder, c. 1870.

own creative vision.[2] The passionate and violent scenes described in Zola's novels appear in a number of Cézanne's paintings executed at around the same time, transformed and assimilated by his romantic imagination. So, since the institution that held the monopoly in artistic training had rejected him, he remained very much on the fringes. Zola, once again, was fully behind him: 'I entirely approve of your idea of coming to work in Paris and then withdrawing to Provence. I see it as a way of resisting the influence of the schools and of developing any originality you may possess.'[3]

This dividing of his time between Paris and Provence became a habit, enabling Cézanne to spend the summers working in his studio at the family home, the Jas de Bouffan. Here, he pursued his pictorial investigations, using various members of his family as models: his Uncle Dominique, of whom he made a number of heavily textured portraits, wearing a variety of costumes; his mother, his sister and his father, of whom, in 1866, he made a particularly masterful portrait.

From the following year onwards, the works reflected to an increasing degree the passion, torment and instability of the apprentice painter. In his search for a personal style, Cézanne was drawn on the one hand to Courbet, who was then at the very height of his fame and from whom he occasionally borrowed certain provocative elements; but on the other, paradoxically, to 'the elegant Manet', a leading figure whose *Olympia* had, to the astonishment of all, been accepted for the Salon of 1865. This success of Manet's undoubtedly inspired Cézanne to turn to a similar theme and to develop even further its potential for scandal: in 1867, he submitted to the Salon a depiction of an orgy scene in a brothel, entitled *The Rum Punch*,[4] that struck the jury as far more obscene and indefensible than had the extreme realism of Manet's *Olympia*. Cézanne's painting sparked such sarcastic re-

marks from the critic Arnold Mortier in *L'Europe* that Zola was moved to reply with the following defence in 12 April 1867 edition of *Le Figaro*: 'This is one of my childhood friends, a young painter whose strong and individual talent I particularly admire.'

The works from this period reflect an occasional interest in religious painting (*The Madeleine*), but a more frequent one in subjects of a violent and ominous nature (*The Abduction, The Murder, The Laying Out*), rendered with a clumsiness that is apparently deliberate. There is no doubt that during this period Cézanne was deeply preoccupied with atrocity, excess and exaggeration. The following year, he was once again rejected by the Salon; this time, however, Degas, Monet, Pissarro, Renoir, Sisley and Manet were accepted, the last with his famous *Portrait of Zola*. Their success was almost certainly due to the presence of Daubigny on the jury.

In a series of articles published in *L'Evénement illustré* during the month of May, Zola attempted to publicize the fine work being produced by these painters, so much of which was in the landscape genre. The terms he employs in his defence of Pissarro are close to those of the doctrine of Naturalism: 'The artist cares for nothing but truth, nothing but fidelity; he places himself before a piece of nature and sets himself the task of interpreting the precise span of its horizons, without adding the slightest embellishment of his own invention; he is

2. See Mary Tomkins Lewis, 'Literature and Cézanne's Early Subjects', in Gowing, *Cézanne: The Early Years* (exhib. cat.), pp.32–40; Mary Louise Krumrine, in *Paul Cézanne. Les baigneuses* (exhib. cat.), pp.33–103; and Theodore Reff, 'Cézanne, Flaubert, St Antony and the Queen of Sheba', pp. 113–25. In most cases, the complete references of works referred to appear in the bibliography at the end of this volume.
3. Cézanne, *Correspondance*, p.106.
4. This painting is now lost; there does exist, however, a work on paper (gouache and watercolour) that gives us some idea of the work's subject and composition (ill. in Gowing, *op. cit.*, pl. 67).

The Abduction, 1867.

neither poet not philosopher, but simply a naturalist, a maker of skies and of lands.'[5] And Monet seems to the critic to possess the same concern for truth: 'He is one of the few painters that knows how to paint water, without foolish transparency, without false reflections. In his work, water is alive, deep – above all, real.'[6] Zola even goes so far as to argue that the work of these artists is the inevitable outcome of the evolution of French painting: 'Our landscapists have broken openly with tradition . . . The classical landscape is dead, killed by life and by truth.'[7]

Cézanne was not entirely indifferent to Zola's naturalist principles, and towards the end of the 1860s he made several forays into a form of realism that none the less retained a certain quality of strangeness. Examples of the works from this period are *Young Girl at the Piano, Portrait of the Painter Achille Emperaire* and *Paul Alexis reading to Émile Zola* (p. 53). As he mentioned in a letter to his friend Numa Coste in late November of 1868,[8] he even considered presenting a landscape to the Salon of 1869 (see p. 51). We do not know for sure, however, if this was the painting that was responsible for his being – yet again – rejected. Openly derisory, he had aspired for some time to the status of *refusé*. In a letter to Pissarro, dated 15 March 1865, he wrote: 'On Saturday we're going to the outfit on the Champs-Elysées to deliver our canvases, which will make the Institute blush with rage and despair.'[9] It was this attitude that, just before the opening of the Salon of 1870, caused Cézanne to become the butt of Parisian caricaturists: in a weekly magazine published by Stock (see p. 12), a cartoonist showed him wearing a

Portrait of Achille Emperaire, c. 1868.

5. Zola, *Mon Salon. Manet* (Paris: Garnier-Flammarion, 1970), p. 147.
6. *Ibid.*, p. 153.
7. *Ibid.*, p.157.
8. Cézanne, *Correspondance*, p.134.
9. *Ibid.*, p.113.

Stock, caricature of Paul Cézanne with the two paintings rejected by the Salon jury of 1870, published in an unidentified Paris newspaper.

heavy 'revolutionary' beard, holding a palette in one hand, brandishing in the other his portrait of the deformed artist Achille Emperaire, and sporting as a pendant earring a painting of a reclining nude that is possibly the *Nu á la puce*, now lost.[10] The artist's foot is firmly placed over a sheet of paper inscribed with the worlds *Pour copie conforme* – a guarantee by the cartoonist that the images appearing in his caricature are (hard though it may be to believe) faithful reproductions of the artist's work.

After ten years of struggling, Cézanne had finally achieved fame, but in the pages of the *Album Stock*! The

paragraph that accompanied the caricature is, however, worth quoting: 'I have the honour to introduce you to your master: M. Cézannes [*sic*]. Cézannes! who? what?? – Cézannes hails from Aix-en-Provence. He is a realist painter and, what is more, a convinced one. But listen to him, rather, telling me in his pronounced Provençal accent. "Yes, my dear Sir, I paint as I see, as I feel – and I have very strong sensations. The others, too, feel and see as I do, but they don't dare . . . they produce Salon pictures . . . I do dare, M. Stock, I do dare . . . I have the courage of my convictions – and *he who laughs last laughs longest*." '[11] Assuming this to be a more or less accurate account of the painter's words, it illustrates clearly something of his complexity as an individual. While the caricature portrays a Cézanne apparently delighted by his mockingly comical imitation of a young Salon aspirant, the text reveals a glimpse of the fundamental motive force underlying his vision as an artist: the 'strong sensations' of which the inadequate expression was to be the source of an almost constant 'starting over'.

Cézanne had succeeded in attracting attention and in inspiring this caricature by taking his paintings to the Palais de l'Industrie on the last day of submission, knowing full well that they would be rejected. He had admitted earlier to his desire to provoke the Salon jury in a letter to his childhood friend Fortuné Marion. When the latter remarked that the artist could not continue for long submitting works of this type to the official exhibition, he received the following sharp response: 'You'll see, I'll chuck stuff like that at them till kingdom come,

10. For a penetrating analysis of the implicit political significance of Cézanne's early work, see Nina Athanassoglou-Kallmyer, 'An Artistic and Political Manifesto for Cézanne', *The Art Bulletin*, vol. LXXIII, no. 3, September 1990. pp.482–92.

11. John Rewald, 'Un article inédit sur Paul Cézanne en 1870', *Arts*, 473, 21 July 1954.

Young Girl at the Piano, 1869–71.

with no respite!'[12] Until 1870 Cézanne's work is hard to classify. This is due to a struggle that was being waged by the artist on two fronts: against the academic tradition, on the one hand, but also, and more importantly, against

Portrait of Émile Zola, 1862.

himself and his incapacity to obtain the results to which he aspired. His painting, rejected by the offical jury, was in any case not in tune with the work of the artists who surrounded Manet each day at the Café Guerbois. Indeed, with his defiantly uncouth manners and apparent

lack of interest in the group's noisy discussions, Cézanne was decidedly odd man out.[13]

This taste for provocation was progressively sublimated in events of some importance. On 31 May 1870, Cézanne appeared as a witness at the marriage of his friend Zola, in Paris. The previous year, he had himself made the acquaintance of a young model, Hortense Fiquet, with whom he was to share his life. On 18 July, at the declaration by France of war on Prussia, Cézanne returned to Aix to avoid conscription. Not wishing to reveal to his family his liaison with Hortense, who had accompanied him, he settled with her in L'Estaque. From there, he visited Aix alone. Following the defeat, he remained in the south for some time, since it would have been impossible to work in Paris during the Commune. When Vollard later questioned him about this period in his life, Cézanne replied: 'Listen, Monsieur Vollard! During the war, I worked a good deal from nature at L'Estaque. Moreover, there are no outstanding events I can tell you about from 1870 and 1871. I divided my time between landscape and the studio.'[14]

Cézanne did not return to Paris until the autumn of 1871. The following January, Hortense gave birth to their son Paul. For a while, he borrowed Guillaumin's studio in order to continue painting. Refused once again by the Salon in 1872, he finally accepted Pissarro's invitation to

12. Cézanne, quoted by Marion in a letter addressed to their mutual friend, the German pianist Heinrich Morstatt. See M. Scolari and A. Barr, 'Cézanne d'aprés les lettres de Marion à Morstatt', *Gazette des Beaux-Arts*, XVII, 1937, p.37.
13. This café, near Manet's studio at 11 Grand-rue-des-Batignolles (now Avenue de Clichy), was a regular meeting-place for a number of artists; among the group were Bazille, Degas, Guillaumin, Guillemet, Renoir and several critics who defended the new painting. Béliard, Cézanne, Monet, Pissarro and Sisley also frequented the café when in Paris.
14. Ambroise Vollard, *Paul Cézanne* (Paris: Éditions Georges Crés et Cie, 1919). p.37.

settle with his family in Pontoise, where the country air could only be beneficial to the new baby. This was the beginning of Cézanne's true apprenticeship as a painter.

Painting from nature with Pissarro

Over the past several years, the group of artists that frequented the Café Guerbois had gradually succeeded in having a few of their paintings accepted by the Salon jury, a jury that had become marginally more open to the work of independent painters but that was just as unpredictable and arbitrary in its choices as ever. That Cézanne was again rejected for the 1870 Salon – the last of the Second Empire – was hardly surprising and could be attributed as much to his behaviour as his art. But the rejection of Monet the same year was less expected, given that his work had been accepted in 1865, 1866, and 1868. It was this event, moreover, that prompted Daubigny and Corot to resign from the jury. The other painters in the group seem to have fared better that year at the hands of this institution usually so unreceptive to innovation. Moreover, the critic Théodore Duret enthusiastically defended the newcomers in the opposition weekly *L'Électeur libre*, expressing a particular liking for the landscapes of Pissarro.

Cézanne was a sufficiently frequent participant in the Café Guerbois meetings to realize the significance of this development for new painting in general. His enforced retreat to Aix and L'Estaque must have provided him with an opportunity to reflect with an open mind on the debates taking place in Paris, and also perhaps to overcome certain deep-seated conflicts that re-emerged continually in his painting. Having channelled at least part of his anguish into a series of three narrative paintings of highly personal content – *The Temptation of St Anthony*

(p. 55), *Le Déjeuner sur l'herbe* and *Pastoral* – Cézanne was free to devote himself entirely to painting from nature. Painting from nature outdoors, something he had done on occasion in the south, might prove, as it had for others, to be a way of being accepted into the Salon. This hope was made all the more real by the new opportunities for

Portrait of Dr Gachet, 1873.

Photograph of Cézanne and Pissarro in Auvers region, c. *1874*.

exhibiting his work that had, since his return to Paris in the autumn of 1871, been opened up by the support of Paul Durand-Ruel.

During the war, the well-known dealer of the Barbizon painters had spent time in London, where, through an intensive cultivation of collectors and the organization of exhibitions, he had succeeded in recruiting a number of English supporters for this type of art. During his stay, Durand-Ruel had been introduced by Daubigny to Monet, who had fled France and was struggling with financial difficulties, and had met and helped Pissarro too. These meetings proved to be decisive for the futures of these artists and of their friends. Since his return to Paris, Durand-Ruel had been buying paintings by Manet, Degas and Monet. Pissarro was even receiving a monthly stipend in exchange for works and was participating in the London exhibitions that the dealer continued to organize. Given the very real possibility of a renewed market interest in so-called 'light' painting, it is not surprising that Cézanne accepted the invitation of Pissarro – well-known for the generosity with which he offered advice and support – and finally spent two years (1872–4) in his company, first in Saint-Ouen-L'Aumône, near Pontoise, and later in Auvers-sur-Oise.[15] Several other painters, moreover, had already left Paris to settle in the country, among them Sisley, who went to Louveciennes, and Monet, who settled in Argenteuil, where he was visited frequently by Renoir.

Starting again, according to new principles, after ten years of a romantic exuberance that had led him into inextricable contradictions, involved Cézanne in a daily struggle with his own nature – a struggle to gain control over his most deep-seated passions and his overflowing imagination. Pissarro's patience helped him to achieve discipline and method, to curb the speed of his work, to submit himself to a painting rather than fling himself headlong into it. The direct contact with nature afforded by painting outdoors seems to have been an essential element in his development. Pissarro must have encouraged Cézanne to force himself to observe the visible in the minutest detail and to slow down his use of the coloured forms to render the wealth he discovered. All his passion was now channelled into his visual perception and, in his efforts to transpose in chromatic values every nuance of light he observed, he began to scrutinize nature with the same intensity that he had once used to explore his own fantasies.

Over the following two years Cézanne's artistic output increased considerably, and it included a large number of landscapes, painted for the most part in the company of Pissarro in the countryside surrounding the towns where they were staying. Each of the many views of houses in Auvers, of winding roads (see p. 59) and of the roofs of Pontoise is an attempt to rise to the double challenge of attaining a much sought-after unity of space while avoiding the fragmentation of forms through an over-use of effects of vibration. Applying himself ever more earnestly to the task, Cézanne went from a dry brush to a palette knife and back to a brush in his efforts to discover exactly the stroke he wanted. For, in spite of Pissarro's suggestions, he had lost nothing of his desire to assert his own individuality. As Pissarro wrote to his son during Cézanne's exhibition at Vollard's gallery in 1895: 'What is interesting is . . . the similarity of certain of the Auvers and Pontoise landscapes to my own. Good Lord, we were

---

15. Pissarro only worked occasionally at the Académie Suisse, where he and Cézanne first met, but he had already undergone formal training, during 1855–6, at the studios of Dagnin, Lehmann and Picot, all professors at the École des Beaux-Arts. He had also had a landscape accepted for the Salon as early as 1859, had his work corrected by the marine painter Anton Melbye, and was acquainted with Corot, Chintreuil and Daubigny. It was thus to a painter of some experience, nine years his senior, that Cézanne turned for help in 1872.

Pissarro, *Portait of Cézanne, 1874.*

always together! But one thing is certain, each of us held on to the only thing that counts – his own "sensation". It would be easy to demonstrate.'[16]

Evidently not satisfied with rendering merely the ephemeral aspects of light, Cézanne aimed at developing a stroke with which he could actually build up volumes, spaces and their interrelationships. This eventually became his central preoccupation as a painter. For the time being, though, Pissarro's style had a predominantly liberating effect on Cézanne's work that he would subsequently put to good use. Moreover, he never denied the crucial role played by Pissarro in his development. Unlike Monet and Renoir, who were fascinated during this period by the capturing of the transitory, Pissarro – as his many preparatory sketches go to show – laid great stress on the sound construction of a landscape.[17] Once the composition was established, he would then proceed to the meticulous application of colour to render what he called the 'atmospheric envelope'. Cézanne, who had been attempting to transpose his sensations directly on to the canvas, almost certainly adopted many elements of Pissarro's method. Indeed, it was perhaps the initial source of his legendary slowness of execution and his tireless quest for solid, ordered construction.

More important, though, than any similarities or differences of style was the deep friendship linking the two men, which had its roots in an entirely mutual respect and admiration that was no doubt largely responsible for Pissarro's 'pedagogical' success. His *Portrait of Cézanne*, painted early in 1874 and kept in his studio until his death, is very revealing of the friendly atmosphere within which this apprenticeship took place. Cézanne's casual attire is that of a painter who works frequently outdoors. On the right-hand side of the painting, to Cézanne's left, Pissarro has juxtaposed one of his own landscapes and a caricature of Courbet – respectively symbols, for his

sitter, of the landscape genre and of the revolt against 'official' painting. Opposite, can be seen a caricature of Adolphe Thiers, President of the Republic, made at the time of the spectacular success of his 1872 loan.[18]

The association of these images with Cézanne cannot have been entirely innocent. Pissarro's anarchistic tendencies would have made him more sympathetic to Courbet than to Thiers. The depiction of Cézanne between the two irreconcilable positions represented by Thiers, the liberal bourgeois, and Courbet, partisan of the Commune, is evidence of a gentle mocking by Pissarro of the contradictions embodied in his friend, who was known for his horror of the political discussions at the Café Guerbois and for a certain lingering 'middle-classness' beneath the uncouth and careless appearance.

But the good Pissarro did more than just accept Cézanne wholeheartedly, with all his contradictions: he contributed indirectly to his financial support. On his monthly trips to Paris, he would take Cézanne – and some of his works – to the paint shop run by Père Tanguy, a man who shared his political views. Père Tanguy would accept the paintings in exchange for tubes of paint and canvas, and then exhibit them in the window of his store. Pissarro also managed to persuade the grocer in Pontoise

16. Camille Pissarro, *Lettres à son fils Lucien* (Paris: Albin Michel, 1950). p.391.
17. See *Pissarro* (Paris: Galerie nationale du Grand Palais, 1981).
18. For a discussion of the images seen in the background of this portrait of Cézanne, see Theodore Reff's excellent article, 'Pissarro's Portrait of Cézanne', *The Burlington Magazine*, vol. CIX, November 1967, pp. 627–30. The caricature of Courbet, by Léonce Petit, had appeared in the 13 June 1867 issue of *Le Hanneton*, at the time of the exhibition of the artist's works at the Alma pavilion during the Exposition Universelle. The drawing of Thiers, by André Gill, was published in *L'Eclipse* on 4 August 1872. It alludes to the massive response of the French people (41 billion francs) to his request for a loan to be used for repaying war indemnities to Prussia and liberating the remaining occupied territories more quickly. The painting by Pissarro has also been identified: it is *Road to Gisors, Père Galien's House*.

where he and Cézanne obtained their supplies to agree to the same arrangement.

Since his move to Auvers-sur-Oise in the autumn, moreover, Cézanne had become friendly with Dr Paul Gachet, an old acquaintance from the Café Guerbois. The doctor, whose practice was in Paris, had recently installed his family in Auvers in an attempt to improve his wife's failing health. He was himself a painter and engraver, and he willingly lent Cézanne his studio and bought a number of his works to contribute towards his support. Among the paintings purchased by Dr Gachet was *A Modern Olympia* (p. 61); apparently executed in the doctor's studio, it depicts the world of a fashionable courtesan.

1874–7: Impressionist or independent?

It was this *Modern Olympia* that Cézanne chose to present at the first exhibition of the Société anonyme des artistes peintres, sculpteurs, graveurs, etc., held from 15 April to 15 May 1874, at 35 Boulevard des Capucines in one of the large spaces lent by the photographer Nadar and transformed for the occasion into a gallery.[19] Cézanne almost certainly felt that this work and the two others mentioned in the catalogue – *The House of the Hanged Man at Auvers-sur-Oise* and *Study: Landscape at Auvers* – represented his work at its most advanced. We can only speculate as to why the artist would have decided to exhibit a genre scene when he had been devoting himself almost exclusively to landscape for the past two years.[20] This exhibition was the first occasion on which Cézanne showed his works in public. Perhaps he had not entirely abandoned his early artistic ambitions. Or perhaps he wanted to live up to his reputation as a *provocateur*, or simply make sure his work did not go unnoticed.

In an attempt to gain publicity, the exhibition organized

Photograph of the house of the hanged man at Auvers-sur-Oise.

by the new association, whose aim was to overcome the major obstacle represented by the repeated injustices meted out by the jury, opened its doors two weeks before the official Salon. It is commonly thought that the Société was attempting to promote a particular aesthetic approach, shared by its members, which reflected neither official standards nor those imposed by the Académie des Beaux-Arts. The list of exhibitors, however, proves that no stylistic criteria governed the choice of works. Most of the particpants were more conventional artists who had already acquired a reputation at the Salon and who were

19. For more on the history of this anonymous society, the motives that prompted its members to organize this exhibition and the reaction of the critics, see Paul Tucker's recent article 'The First Impressionist Exhibition in Context', *The New Painting* (The Fine Arts Museum of San Francisco, 1986), pp.93–123, and Jean-Paul Bouillon, 'Sociétés d'artistes et institutions officielles dans la seconde moitié du XIXe siécle', *Romantisme*, no. 54, 1986, pp.89–113.

20. Cézanne continued regularly to paint genre scenes – for the most part erotic in nature – until 1880. He returned to the *Déjeuner sur l'herbe* and *Temptation of St Anthony* themes, and also made works on the subject of *Bathsheba* and *L'Eternel féminin*, the latter even reappearing as the subject of a water-colour dating from the end of the 1880s.

invited – at Degas's insistence – to give the exhibition credibility. The proponents of 'independence', called subsequently by critics the 'Impressionists', made up only about a quarter of the exhibitors, which probably

Pissarro setting out to Paint, 1872–6.

accounts to some degree for the considerable attention they received.

The principal aim of these artists in mounting the exhibition was to gain an opening into the art market that did not involve having to go through a dealer and that remained outside the Salon 'network'. Théodore Duret advised Pissarro not to take part, but to persevere in submitting works to the Salon in the hope of eventually – like Manet – being accepted. Manet himself, anxious not to damage his newly acquired reputation, declined the Société's invitation. But Pissarro remained loyal to his friends and even persuaded them to include works by Guillaumin, Béliard and Cézanne. Because of the scandalous nature of some of his earlier works, getting the association to agree to include Cézanne was no easy task. But no one had seen his recent paintings, and Pissarro was soon proven right: the small landscape entitled *The House of the Hanged Man at Auvers-sur-Oise*, whose clear and disciplined execution testifies to its author having put his recently learned lessons to good use, was purchased during the exhibition by a major collector of the new painting, Count Doria.

At the time of the exhibition, Cézanne had not seen his parents for three years, probably because the small allowance he received, on which he now had to support a wife and child, did not permit it. At the end of May he left for Aix, without even taking time to shake Pissarro's hand (as he wrote to his friend on 24 June 1874). His wife and son, whose existence he had still not revealed to his father, remained in Paris. By September he was back in the capital and, if we are to believe the tone of a letter written to his mother, apparently calm and confident of the future: 'I know that he [Pissarro] has a good opinion of me, and I have a very good opinion of myself. I'm beginning to think that I'm better than those around me, and you know that my own good opinion of my work has

Entrance of a Farm at Auvers, c. *1873.*

not been easily won. I have to work constantly, but not to obtain a finish, which pleases only idiots . . . Believe me, my moment will come and I will have admirers far more fervent and convinced than those seduced by mere appearance.' He goes on to add that 'sales are very bad, the bourgeois are hanging on to their money for dear life, but it'll pass'.[21]

This new assurance is somewhat surprising. The economic situation alluded to by Cézanne in his letter was linked to the difficult early years of the Third Republic,

which had been accompanied by a major financial and administrative reorganization. The resulting economic slow-down had a drastic effect on the art market, and from 1874 Durand-Ruel was obliged to cut back on his purchasing. After having seemingly 'discovered their niche', as Pissarro put it, Cézanne and his friends found themselves once more in a precarious situation that was to be further aggravated by subsequent events.

In December 1874, for example, the general lack of success of the venture led the members of the Société anonyme, under the presidency of Renoir, to vote for its dissolution. The following year, hoping to overcome their financial difficulties, Renoir, Monet, Sisley and Morisot held an auction of their works at the Hôtel Drouot. But the event led only to fresh disappointment and the results were catastrophic. The hostility of the general public did nothing to encourage potential buyers, and the paintings went for ridiculous prices. Durand-Ruel, who attended the auction in the capacity of expert, was powerless to save the situation.

Although Cézanne did not submit any paintings to the auction, he did benefit from it in an unexpected way. One of the few people to buy works at the Hôtel Drouot was a newcomer called Victor Chocquet. This customs inspector, already a keen collector of Delacroix, took a liking to Renoir's work and bought several of his paintings. A short time later, Chocquet accompanied Renoir on a visit to Père Tanguy's shop, where he became an enthusiastic convert to Cézanne's art. This was the beginning of a long friendship between the collector and these artists, and Chocquet became an ardent defender of the new painting, especially Cézanne's. (When Chocquet's collection was sold after his death in 1899, it included thirty-

21. Cézanne, *Correspondance,* p.148.

Portrait of Victor Choquet, 1876–7.

one paintings by Cézanne). Moreover, his support came at a particularly welcome time, for a tightening up of the Salon admission criteria – Manet was refused in 1876 – had put government backing completely beyond the reach of the artists who defended a new aesthetic vision.

Once again, they were obliged to adopt the strategy of a group exhibition. The event was held in April 1876, one month before opening of the Salon, in Durand-Ruel's establishment on rue Le Peletier. Cézanne, who had spent the winter in L'Estaque, may have regretted not taking part, for in spite of the harsh reviews of certain critics, the venture proved far from disastrous. Back in Paris, he wrote to his parents following a visit to Guillaumin: ' . . . He told me that the exhibition organized last April by the painters on our side was very successful . . . Not only was the three thousand francs reached, but the fifteen hundred francs advanced in equal shares by the artists was refunded to them, plus a three-franc dividend, which isn't much, it's true. It's a pretty good beginning.' Hoping no doubt to convince his parents to advance him the sum needed to participate in the next event, Cézanne is clearly gratified to be able to continue: 'According to Guillaumin, I am one of three new members scheduled to join and I was very warmly defended by Monet at a dinner meeting when a certain Lepic spoke out against my admittance.'[22]

In April 1877, then, Cézanne took part in the most cohesive of the exhibitions organized by the group that accepted for this occasion only the label given to them by critics for the past several years: the 'Impressionists'. Meticulously planned by Gustave Caillebotte, the exhibition included the work of only eighteen artists, but represented each of them much more widely than before – the catalogue indicates a total of 241 works.[23] Most of the sixteen paintings submitted by Cézanne belonged to Chocquet, who, according to contemporary accounts, spent whole days in the exhibition rooms trying to convince visitors of the validity of the art on view. Once again, however, the political disorder that continued to reign in France proved fatal to speculative investment. While the exhibition owes some of its fame to the extraordinary number of caricatures it inspired in satirical journals, a careful reading of the reviews indicates that reaction was generally more positive than might have been expected. Nevertheless, the hoped-for financial success was not achieved.

While the critics showed themselves slightly more receptive to certain members of the group, Cézanne's works continued to arouse either violent hostility or total derision. The only positive remarks about him were made by Georges Rivière in his short-lived publication *L'Impressionniste, journal d'art*. There is nothing to indicate Cézanne's reaction to this new attack: deep disappointment, re-assessment, indifference? One thing we do know, however – it did not prompt him to give up. 'I go every day to the park in Issy, where I make a few studies', he wrote. 'And I'm not too dissatisfied, but it seems that deep dejection reigns in the Impressionist camp. They're not exactly rolling in money, and the works are just piling up. We live in very troubled times, and I don't know when poor painting will regain a little of its lustre.'[24]

---

22. *Ibid.*, p.155.
23. As Durand-Ruel's exhibition space was already reserved, Caillebotte had the idea of renting a large apartment situated at 6 rue Le Peletier, opposite the gallery. See Richard Brettell, 'The First Exhibition of Impressionist Painters', in *The New Painting* (see n. 19), pp.189–202.
24. Cézanne, *Correspondance*, p.158. Since the end of the Second Empire, France had been struggling to extricate itself from a political instability caused by constant clashes between conservative monarchists and left-wing republicans. After the major crisis of 1877, the Republicans finally won the day. Following hard upon the war, these political battles led inevitably to a slow-down in the economy, for middle-class traders and business people hesitated to invest during a period of unrest. The Exposition Universelle of 1878 marked the beginning of a long-awaited economic recovery.

Photograph of Cézanne setting out to paint in the region of
Auvers-sur-Oise, c. *1874*.

He continued to work for a while longer in the environs of Paris and then returned south at the beginning of the following year. As he explained to Octave Maus some time later, it was not disdain that led him to refuse to participate in exhibitions. 'I would say on this subject that the many studies I had undertaken had given me such negative results that, dreading all-too-justified criticism, I had resolved to work in silence, until the time when I felt able to defend theoretically the results of my efforts.'[25]

It seems clear that Impressionism was only a stage, decisive but short-lived, in Cézanne's artistic development. Unhampered by any stylistic labels, participating in none of the group's subsequent exhibitions (the last of these rather sporadic events was held in 1886), working alone at perfecting everything he had learnt from Pissarro, and still rejected by the Salon in spite of repeated submissions, Cézanne inevitably became the most independent of painters.

Parallel to his painting

Since the month of August 1877, Cézanne had been planning to spend the winter in the south. It was a visit that required more careful planning than usual, for this time he wanted Hortense and their son Paul to accompany him, but discreetly, since he had still not revealed the relationship to his father for fear of losing his monthly allowance. It was finally not until the following March that Cézanne successfully installed his family in Marseilles, while he stayed in L'Estaque. However, dashing back and forth between the two places and avoiding paternal displeasure by still making regular visits to Aix proved more complicated than he had imagined, and it was not long before his father learned of the existence of his grandson from a third party. Towards the end of March, Cézanne confided his difficulties to Zola: 'It looks as

though pretty soon I'm going to have to find a way of supporting myself, if only I can. Things are very strained between my father and me, and there's a risk that I'll lose my allowance entirely. A letter I received from Monsieur Chocquet, in which he speaks of "Madame Cézanne and little Paul", has served to make my position quite clear to my father, who was actually already very watchful and full of suspicion, and who did not hesitate to open the letter addressed to me and read it, even though it was clearly marked "Mons. Paul Cézanne – painter".'[26]

A difficult year, then, taken up for the most part by strategic moves from one place to another, the details of which can be traced through his correspondence. Zola, following the enormous success of L'Assommoir, had recently bought a house in Médan on the banks of the Seine, just down river from Saint-Germain-en-Laye, and Cézanne earnestly beseeched his childhood friend to help him out by sending money directly to Hortense that would make up for the reduction in his father's allowance. Cézanne's insistent and repeated requests for aid ceased the following year – probably an indication that his family was coming to terms with the situation.

All this tension does not seem to have had a very positive effect on his painting. 'I am working, without much result – too far from the general meaning', he wrote on 14 April 1878. Few canvases are known to date from this period. Since his work in Pontoise and Paris, Cézanne had been trying to arrive at a technique that would allow him to integrate each stroke into an overall structure. Until this point, he had been pursuing these purely plastic investigations in a series of exclusively 'made-up' paintings, executed without the use of live models. His many studies of Bathers, a good number of whom are

---

25. *Ibid.*, p.229.
26. *Ibid.*, pp.160–1.

female, are an attempt to respond to one of painting's most important challenges: the depiction of the nude human figure in a natural setting. For it is here that the problem of spatial unity makes itself most acutely felt. Cézanne's treatment of this theme, to which he would return again and again, finally culminated in the large compositions that date from after 1900.

In April 1879 he returned to Paris – once again unsuccessfully submitting works to the Salon – and settled in Melun, no doubt attracted by the calm atmosphere and fine light of L'Île de France. 'I am still struggling to find my artistic voice', he wrote, 'Nature presents me with the most enormous problems.'[27] He visited Zola at Médan in the autumn, and again the following year. He also saw something of his fellow natives of Provence, Numa Coste and Paul Alexis, and even renewed ties with old Café Guerbois acquaintances, Duret and Guillemet. It was around then that he met J.K. Huysmans, at that time an enthusiastic member of Zola's circle, who recommended to him a number of novels that the artist appears to have appreciated greatly. He certainly lost no time in sharing his interest with Pissarro when he met up with him again in Pontoise, in the summer of 1881: 'I see Pissarro quite often, and I've lent him Huysmans's book, which he loves. I'm working on several studies, some in sunlight, some not.'[28]

It was during this period that he met Paul Gauguin, who, still working as a bank employee, spent a few days' holiday painting with Pissarro. Gauguin was extremely interested in Cézanne's work and even purchased a few of his paintings from Père Tanguy's shop, including a view of Médan Castle (p. 71) and a magnificent *Still Life with Compotier*[29] that had at least as much effect on his painting as Pissarro's advice. Cézanne even accused Gauguin of trying to 'steal his little sensations'.

During the period spent on the Île de France, Cézanne

Bend in the Road, 1879–82.

turned again to certain themes that had interested him earlier (see, for example, *Bend in the Road*, 1879–82, Museum of Fine Arts, Boston). But he also embarked confidently on a number of new subjects – *Fontainebleau under the Snow* (Museum of Modern Art, New York), *Poplars* (Musée d'Orsay, Paris) and *The Bridge at Maincy* (Musée d'Orsay, Paris [p. 69]) – in which the structure he so eagerly sought was at least partially achieved through a more methodical handling involving small brushstrokes placed parallel to one another. Without there being any major rupture, a gradual but noticeable change was taking place in his work, one that held a wealth of possibilities for the future.

27. *Ibid.*, p.185.
28. *Ibid.*, p.200.
29. This still life, which Gauguin kept at least until 1890, appears in the background of his own *Portrait of a Woman*, now at the Art Institute of Chicago.

Towards the end of the year, Cézanne returned once again to Aix. This constant moving about had had the effect of making him an almost legendary figure. Avoiding the gatherings at the Café de la Nouvelle Athénes (which after the war had replaced the Café Guerbois as the artists' meeting-place), steering clear of fashionable bourgeois society, living largely outside Paris, Cézanne inspired more rumours as the result of his 'antisocial' behaviour than of his painting. In a short story published posthumously in 1881, Edmond Duranty sketched an unkind but not especially surprising portrait of the painter in the guise of a character called Maillobert, described as a 'vulgar dauber' who painted 'with a spoon'.[30]

From 1883 on, apart from brief visits to friends – Renoir in La Roche-Guyon, Zola in Médan and Chocquet in Normandy – Cézanne remained completely isolated in Aix for a period of several years. He pursued unceasingly his search for what he called a 'subject to analyse', by which he meant a compelling subject that enabled him to construct a complex and highly analytic pictorial composition in which all the various elements

Photograph of the environs of Aix, with Sainte-Victoire in the background.

were closely interrelated. 'I have some nice views here,' he wrote from L'Estaque, 'but they don't quite make it as "subjects".'[31] None the less, his rendering of these views has given us paintings of the most astonishing density (pp. 79 and 83), a density that succeeds in suggesting depth yet remains within the flat surface of the canvas.

It was during this period that Cézanne created his first great Provençal landscapes: the eternally recurring Mont Sainte-Victoire (pp. 91 and 93) scenes of the areas surrounding Gardanne, Bellevue and Beaurecueil, and views through the chestnut trees of the Jas de Bouffan; views, also, of the Jas de Bouffan itself – for more than forty years one of the artist's favourite places – with its pond, its trees, its long, shady avenue and its farmhouse (see pp. 85–89). When the house was renovated in 1881, Cézanne had a small studio added and here, in addition to the painting sessions out of doors, he spent long and patient hours executing a large number of still lifes.

During these years a storm was gathering on the Parisian horizon that would put an end to a long friendship. Since the appearance in *Le Voltaire*, in 1880, of Zola's reviews of the Salon, there was no longer any doubt that the once-ardent defender of the new painting was disappointed by the results of so many years of effort. 'The real misfortune', he wrote, 'is that no artist of this group has achieved powerfully and definitively the new formula which, scattered through their works, they all offer. The formula is there, endlessly diffused; but nowhere, among any of them, is it to be found applied by a master. They are all forerunners. The man of genius is not yet born'[32] He deplored the fact that 'Monsieur Paul

30. Edmond Duranty, *Le Pays des Arts* (Paris: Charpentier, 1881), pp.316–20.
31. Cézanne, *Correspondance*, p.211.
32. Zola, *Mon Salon. Manet* (Paris: Garnier-Flammarion, 1970), p.377.

Cézanne, who has the makings of a great painter . . . is still struggling with problems of execution . . . '

To start with, Cézanne did not take personally the reproaches aimed at the Impressionists, aware, as he was, of his individuality and originality. It took him some time to grasp fully the decline in Zola's enthusiasm for his work, and he continued to correspond with the writer on very cordial terms until 1886. He also continued to make amicable visits to Médan and to keep up with Zola's novels, which his friend invariably sent him as soon as they were published. But one day Cézanne received a copy of Zola's *L'Oeuvre*, a *roman à clef* based on their shared youth in Aix and describing the rise, fall and eventual suicide of a failed genius, Parisian painter Claude Lantier.

In spite of the fact that the imaginary painter's fate was determined largely by his membership to the Rougan-Macquart 'family', Pissarro, Renoir and Manet all re-

Sketches and caricatures on a letter from Cézanne to Émile Zola, *July 1889*.

proached Zola with having seriously misdrawn this character to whom they felt so linked, believing firmly that the book would have a negative effect on their reputations.[33] In Cézanne's case, the memories evoked were too real for him to accept seeing them as merely associated with the tragic destiny of a failure, even though the character's career in no way mirrored his own. The friendship was over. He wrote, politely but coldly, thanking 'the author of the Rougon-Macquarts' and saying that the book recalled 'times gone by'.[34] The short note, dated 4 April 1886, was apparently the last Cézanne ever addressed to Zola. He no longer sustained any illusions about Zola's incomprehension of the painter's anguish – anguish that he had himself always succeeded in overcoming.

On 28 April 1886, for reasons that remain unclear, Cézanne married Hortense Fiquet in a ceremony attended by his parents. Whether the marriage was carried out in deference to the bourgeois principles of Louis-Auguste Cézanne in what were to be the last months of his life is not known. However, his death, a short time later, put an end to the artist's financial worries once and for all. In just a few months, then, Cézanne's personal story took a major turn, the regularization of his marital status and his inheritance of the family fortune both serving to establish him in a decidedly less marginal social position. As Merleau-Ponty has so perceptively remarked: 'It is certainly true that the life does not *explain* the work, but it is equally true that the two are linked.'[35] Henceforth, Cézanne had no further need to struggle for his independence and could put all his efforts into struggling for his art.

33. For more on the artists' reactions, see John Rewald, 1986, pp. 161–9.
34. Cézanne, *Correspondance*, p.225.
35. Maurice Merleau-Ponty, 'Le doute de Cézanne', in *Sens et Non-sens* (Paris: Nagel, 1948, p.34.

Avenue at Jas de Bouffan, 1884–7.

Solitude: the obsession with painting

For the next two years, Cézanne lived in complete isolation at the Jas de Bouffan. He saw few visitors and kept completely aloof from the numerous avant-garde movements that, in Paris, were following one upon the other at an increasingly frenetic rate. The extraordinary level of activity can be deduced from a single sample year: 1886 saw the eighth and last Impressionist exhibition, the emergence of Seurat and the 'Neo-Impressionist' group and their defence by critic Felix Fénéon, and the rise of Symbolism with the publication of Moréas's 'Manifesto' in *Le Figaro*.

Since no letters written by Cézanne between May 1886

Landscape, 1884–7.

and June 1889 have come down to us, we know nothing of his reaction to these events. However, his last letter prior to this period (11 May 1886), written to his friend Chocquet, in whom he had complete confidence, contains some very candid remarks that concern his own vision of himself and throw a good deal of light on his introversion:

So, I do not wish to be a burden to you, I mean to your state of mind, but since Delacroix has served as an intermediary between you and me, I would like to say this: that I should have wished to possess the intellectual equilibrium that characterizes you and permits you to achieve so surely the desired end. Your kind letter, together with Mme Chocquet's, offers proof of a great equilibrium of human faculties. So, since I am struck by this serenity, I am mentioning it to you. Fate did not bless me with the same equanimity; it is the only regret I have about the things of this world . . .'[36]

Cézanne was in constant doubt about his capacity to 'achieve the desired end' and he envied Chocquet his 'serenity'. And yet the motive was there, pushing him constantly to continue the exhausting battle – a battle which, because of the extreme difficulty of transposing landscape with veracity, was almost invariably lost before it was begun. 'In closing,' the artist went on, 'I should tell you that I am still painting and that there are treasures to be taken out of this countryside, which has not yet found an interpreter equal to the wealth it offers.'[37] This dilemma, which had been at the very heart of Cézanne's artistic project since he had resolved to turn his back on his own fantasies and face the world, had its roots in the fundamental ambiguity of all perception. As Merleau-Ponty observed, 'The world is that which I perceive, but its absolute proximity, as soon as it is examined and expressed, becomes also, inexplicably, irremediably far off.'[38]

Direct confrontation with nature was undoubtedly a source of passionate interest to Cézanne, but he was only too aware of the difficulties it involved and he returned periodically to the execution of still life studies, which had the advantage of offering a greater stability. He arranged these subjects with enormous care, ensuring that they each constituted a new and genuine challenge. The total immobility offered by a still life was also demanded of the sitters by Cézanne for his many portraits. His slowness of execution meant, moreover, that each work required endless sittings. The complete absence of expression on his subjects' faces has often been noted: in the portraits of Madame Cézanne, for example, and of various peasants

working on his estate, but also in the paintings depicting Gustave Geffroy, who wrote favourably about his work, and of Ambroise Vollard, who organized his first one-man exhibition.

For Cézanne, these subjects provided him with a pretext to paint, to construct an image, to bring it into being on the canvas, impressive and monumental, rather than a chance to delve into the psychology of individuals. The movement or lack of it in the person represented is derived entirely from the pictorial surface. The subject-matter of the work is painting itself. This attitude of Cézanne's to portraiture explains his reply, reported afterwards by Ambroise Vollard, when – after hundreds of sittings for a portrait – the dealer pointed out two little uncovered spots of canvas on one of the hands: 'If the copy I am making at the Louvre turns out well, perhaps tomorrow I will be able to find the exact tone to cover up those spots. You must understand, Monsieur Vollard, if I put something there by guesswork, I might have to paint the whole canvas over starting from that point!'[39]

In 1888, probably to please Hortense, who was bored in Aix, Cézanne settled once again in Paris, finding lodgings near his friend Guillaumin. He returned frequently to the Louvre to sketch, and painted in the countryside around Paris, either at Chantilly or at Alfort, a town located at the junction of the Seine and the Marne. Through the intervention of his principal collector, Victor Chocquet, one of his works – *The House of the Hanged Man* – was included in the Centennale de l'art français held as part of the Exposition Universelle of

36. Cézanne, *Correspondance*, p.226.
37. *Ibid.*, p.227.
38. Merleau-Ponty, *Le visible et l'invisible* (Paris: Gallimard-NEF, 1964), p.23.
39. P.M. Doran (ed.), *Conversations avec Cézanne* (Paris: Macula, 1978). p.8.

1889. The following year, Cézanne accepted Octave Maus's invitation to exhibit three canvases with Les XX, in Brussels. But his work as a whole remained generally unknown, except to the few who patronized the shop owned by Père Tanguy, still at that time Cézanne's only 'dealer'.

The critics' view

In spite of the distance Cézanne had deliberately put between himself and the artistic circles of Paris, his name began to attract attention towards the end of the 1880s. His loyal friend Pissarro, perhaps the only person to have truly believed in his genius, helped to convince Huysmans of his worth. This critic, well known for the harshness of his reviews, devoted several paragraphs to Cézanne in the 4 August 1888 issue of *La Cravache parisienne* (the paragraphs were reprinted the following year in his book *Certains*). Cézanne's inexplicable deformations of traditional perspective earned him a number of labels, including that of 'the artist with diseased retinas'. The text, however, is striking not for its reiteration of current views but for the accuracy of its observations:

> In full light, in porcelain fruit dishes or on white tablecloths, pears and apples that are coarse, crude, fashioned with a trowel, textured by thumb-smears. From close up a furious plastering of vermilion and of yellow, of green and of blue: to the side, in the middle, fruit fit for the windows of Chevet, luscious, tasty-looking, tempting fruit.
>
> And facts hitherto overlooked become evident, strange and real tones, areas of singular authenticity, nuances of drapery, vassals to the shadows cast by the curves of the fruit and scattered in possible and lovely

Puget's Cupid, 1886–9.

> blues, all of which make these paintings pioneers if we compare them to elegantly traditional still lifes, where the frontal elements stand out brilliantly against unintelligibly murky grounds.
>
> And outdoor landscape sketches, rough drafts that come to nothing, drawings whose freshness is ruined by over-painting, childlike and barbaric outlines and, as well, unbelievable imbalances: houses leaning to one side, as if tipsy; crooked fruit in drunken bowls; naked

Hat. Flowers in a carafe, 1892–6.

bathers, contoured by crazy lines but imbued, to the glory of the eye, with the fire of a Delacroix, without refinement of vision or execution, whipped by a fever of jumbled colours that scream thickly on a weighed-down, drooping canvas!

In sum, a revealing colourist, who has contributed more than the late Manet to the Impressionist movement, an artist with diseased retinas, who, in the exasperated apperception of his vision, has discovered the prodromes of new art; thus may we resume this too-ignored painter, Monsieur Cézanne.[40]

This passage, full of insight and even premonition in its understanding of elements in the works that anticipated a new art, represented Cézanne's first positive review, the first occasion on which – despite certain reservations – his stature as an artist was recognized.

In 1891, the young painter Émile Bernard, a member of the group surrounding Gauguin, had not yet met Cézanne. All he knew of the older artist was what he had learned from his fellows and from Père Tanguy. Bernard nevertheless succeeded in drawing a remarkably accurate verbal portrait of Cézanne, which appeared in the weekly publication *Les Hommes D'Aujourd'hui*.[41] His words echo, even today, with an astonishing clairvoyance. Cézanne, he said, 'opens up for art the unexpected doorway to painting for it's own sake'. The following year, Georges Lecomte devoted a page of highly favourable comments to the artist in his essay entitled *L'Art impressionniste* and granted Cézanne a unique position within the Impressionist group.[42] The critic spoke of the 'marvellous instinct' that produced 'studies of nature, sometimes so unerring as to cause confusion' but that remained 'always noble, even in the representation of the most ordinary objects'. In spite of its lack of polish, its unfinished, crude look, Cézanne's work was recognized for its 'sincerity'. Finally, two texts

by Gustave Geffroy, published in 1893 and 1894, emphasized Cézanne's 'original nature' and described him as 'some kind of a precursor of a new art'.[43]

In December of 1895, encouraged by Pissarro, Monet and Renoir, the young dealer Ambroise Vollard, who had opened a gallery on the rue Lafitte in 1894, held a major exhibition of Cézanne's work. The show (which consisted of 150 paintings, divided into three groups shown in rotation) led to the immediate 'discovery' of the *oeuvre* of this 'mysterious man from Provence', this friend of Zola whom Paris had chosen to ignore for almost twenty years. 'We might have begun to wonder, as we do about Homer and Shakespeare, whether Cézanne had really existed', wrote Arséne Alexandre in his review of the exhibition for *Le Figaro* – a review he artfully entitled 'Claude Lantier'.[44] Cézanne, who had invariably been faced with a total lack of comprehension, did not at first receive the unanimous approbation of the critics. Far from it. But, despite the hesitations of reviewers like Camille Mauclair and Thiebault-Sisson, the worst hurdles were over; with an acuity we cannot help but admire, Geffroy predicted 'He'll end up in the Louvre'. And in the *Revue Blanche*, Thadée Natanson published the most comprehensive article of the period, in which he gave full credit to Cézanne for his role as artistic pioneer.[45]

40. J.K. Huysmans, *L'Art moderne/Certains* (Paris: UGE, 1975), coll. 10/18. pp.308–9.
41. Émile Bernard, 'Paul Cézanne', *Les Hommes d'Aujourd'hui*, 1891, no. 387.
42. Georges Lecomte, *L'Art impressionniste d'aprés la collection privée de M. Durand-Ruel* (Paris: Chamerot et Remouard, 1892), pp. 28–9.
43. Gustave Geffroy, 'L Impressionnisme', *Revue Encyclopédique*, December 1893, column 1223; 'Histoire de l'Impressionnisme', *La Vie artistique* (Paris: Dentu, 1894), vol. 3, pp.249–60.
44. Arséne Alexandre, 'Claude Lantier', *Le Figaro*, 9 December 1895.
45. Thadée Natanson, 'Paul Cézanne', *Revue Blanche*, vol. IX, no. 62, December 1895, pp.496–500.

The Boy in the Red Waistcoat, 1890–5.

The final decade

His association with Vollard (see p. 119) was largely responsible for the increased diffusion of Cézanne's work and the resurgence of the critical debate surrounding it.[46] Interest in his painting was no longer restricted to the small but loyal group of friends from the Impressionist days. Henceforth, Degas, Renoir, Monet and Pissarro, who purchased his work enthusiastically for their own collections, were joined by major collectors such as Paris Deputy Denys Cochin, Florentine Egisto Fabbri (who possessed sixteen of Cézanne's paintings by 1899) and French industrialist Auguste Pellerin. And as the prices steadily rose, Vollard himself purchased more and more: each time Cézanne left one of his temporary studios in the Paris area, Vollard hastened to buy up its entire contents.

This belated success had no effect at all on Cézanne's habits, and he continued to travel regularly back and forth between Aix and the capital. He was increasingly drawn to themes of the south, however, and in his quest for spots less spoiled than L'Estaque and Gardanne, whose landscapes were fast filling up with industrial smoke-stacks, he frequented the disused quarry at Bibémus, east of Aix, where he rented a cabin to store his painting material. The quarry's ochre-coloured rockfaces, overrun with thick, Mediterranean vegetation since its abandon, provided him with many subjects. The road to Le Tholonet, bordered with umbrella pines, also offered a closer view of the Mont Sainte-Victoire. In his constant search for isolated landscapes he discovered – no doubt during a painting trip – the property known as Château-Noir, situated halfway between Aix and Le Tholonet. Since the death of his mother in October 1897, the family residence at the Jas de Bouffan had become something of a burden, much larger than he needed and also, perhaps, too filled

The quarry at Bibémus, c. *1950*.

with memories. The property was eventually put up for sale in 1899 in order to settle his father's estate and divide the proceeds between the painter and his two sisters.

It was at this point that Cézanne made an offer to buy Château-Noir, a proposal that was refused. The owners did agree, however, to rent him a small room in which to store his canvases and other equipment and gave him permission to work on the thickly-wooded property whenever he wished (see pp. 115, 117, 129). The terrace offered a particularly splendid view of Mont Sainte-Victoire. As his wife and son spent most of their time in Paris, Cézanne took living-quarters for himself in Aix, at 23 rue Boulegon, where he set up a temporary studio in the attic. Finally, in 1901, he acquired a piece of land on the road to Les Lauves, north of Aix, where he built a studio big enough to take the large compositions of

46. After the death of Père Tanguy in 1894, Cézanne was without a dealer. After his first one-man exhibition, which was held at Vollard's gallery in 1895 and organized through the intermediary of his son Paul, Vollard visited the painter the following year in Aix. It was then that be became Cézanne's official agent.

Mont Sainte-Victoire, seen from the terrace at Château-Noir, c. *1935.*

bathers that he was planning (see pp. 131, 137). Walking through the countryside to the crest of Les Lauves, he found a new and breathtakingly panoramic view of Mont Sainte-Victoire; rising out of the plain, more majestic than ever, it was to become the subject to which he would return most frequently during these final years (see pp. 127, 133, 135). When the heat of the mistral discouraged him from climbing up to this special spot, he could work on the terrace in front of his studio, in the shade of the linden tree, with a fine view of the town of Aix.

Judging by his wide range of correspondents and the many 'conversations' published subsequently, Cézanne's legendary misanthropy seems to have diminished somewhat by this time. From 1896 on, he allowed his solitude to be punctuated by visits from a number of young admirers with whom he was able to discuss theories about art. Several were from Aix, Including Émile Solari, son of the painter's friend Philippe, and the poet Joachim Gasquet, who introduced Cézanne to his own compan-

ions, Louis Aurenche, Edmond Jaloux and Léo Larguier. His meetings with these young people at at the cafés of the Cours Mirabeau and their visits to the rue Boulegon represented for Cézanne an opportunity to develop a new and easier relationship with the inhabitants of his home town; his contact with his own generation had always been extremely uncomfortable.

The studio at Les Lauves, c. *1904.*

His other visitors were all young artists: Charles Camoin, from Marseilles, who met Cézanne in 1901 while doing his military service in Aix, and in particular Émile Bernard, who spent a month with Cézanne in February 1904, following his return from Egypt.[47]

---

47. Bernard, who had worked at Pont-Aven with Gauguin, aligned himself for a time with the Nabis in Paris and then began to advocate a return to the Renaissance ideal – an approach that paralleled his increasing religious fervour. In 1893, he set off on a long tour of Italy and the Middle East, finally settling in Egypt, where he remained for eleven years.

'Yesterday I went to Aix to see Cézanne', wrote Bernard. 'He's an elderly man, simple, a bit suspicious and strange. As he was just setting off to work, I accompanied him. He spoke to me in a friendly fashion, repeating over and over again "Life is terrible".'[48] Bernard, who wished to 'get to the bottom' of Cézanne and 'reveal his method to later generations', succeeded in gaining the old man's confidence and in prompting him to talk about a number of subjects, including his views on painting, his attitude to nature and to the old masters, and his relationship with Impressionism and Pisarro.

After Bernard's departure, their exchange continued in a series of nine letters which contain the most reliable statements by Cézanne on painting that have come down to us – statements that were sometimes transformed by posterity into theories.[49] Cézanne himself admitted that 'one can . . . with Bernard, develop theories indefinitely, for he has a reasoning mind'.[50] Cézanne, though, was not naturally inclined towards this type of speculation and

A farm near Gardanne, c. *1935.*

always formulated the answers to his correspondent's eager questions in very simple terms. Suspicious of the 'literary spirit that often diverts the painter from his true path', he constantly emphasized the importance of the concrete study of nature, believing that 'a strong sensation of nature . . . is the essential foundation of any concept of art'.

It is important to study Cézanne's propositions as a whole and to avoid taking out of context individual remarks of an apparently more theoretical nature. It is generally accepted today, for example, that Cézanne's famous admonition to 'see in nature the cylinder, the sphere, the cone, putting everything in proper perspective . . .' is simply a reference to academic principles. Abundantly clear, even then, was the fact that Cézanne's central preoccupation was 'the practice of painting', and it was the primal importance of this practice, transcending all theory, that he constantly recalled to Bernard. Thus, on 25 July 1904, he wrote: 'I am sorry we cannot be together, for I do not want to be right in theory, but in nature.'[51] And, in his final letter to the younger artist, dated 21 September 1906, Cézanne wondered:

Will I arrive at my long-sought goal? I hope so; but while it is not achieved there remains a vague malaise, which will only disappear when I reach the port by creating something that works out better than in the

48. Émile Bernard, letter to his mother dated 5 February 1904, in *Conversations avec Cézanne* (see n. 39), p.24.
49. All other direct reports must be treated with the greatest circumspection: several writers, like Vollard, seriously mishandled their sources; others, like Gasquet, actually 'fabricated' conversations designed to throw light on the personality of Cézanne; they are all after-the-fact interpretations that can only be used in conjunction with detailed critical annotations. On this subject, see the excellent work by Michael Doran, *Conversations avec Cézanne*, 1978.
50. Cézanne, *Correspondance*, p.327.
51. *Ibid.*, p.304.

Photograph of Cézanne by Émile Bernard on the hill at Les Lauves, *1904*.

you, this constant obsession with reaching a goal.[52]

Unused to manipulating abstract concepts in a logically consistent way, Cézanne expressed himself somewhat elliptically, and his meaning remains sometimes obscure. 'I am', he confessed, 'only a humble painter and the paint-brush is the means of expression bestowed on me by heaven. So having ideas and developing them is not my business.'[53] The two basic foundation-stones of his painting were complete obedience to an exhaustive observation of nature and the development of a technique permitting the transcription of 'colour sensations that bring light'. Émile Bernard had grasped this at his very first visit: 'Individuality strikes him as necessary for any creator, and what art amounts to, for him, is "The optical vision" or technique. He has developed a very interesting system of grading colours that he wants to perfect. He sees everything as little bits of colour.'[54] Cézanne was attempting to 'give the image of what we see, leaving aside what appeared before us' – he was trying, in other words, to create an image stripped of all the traditional conventions and codes of representation.

The paintings produced in the last years of Cézanne's life, many of which remain unfinished, were invariably the result of an extremely laborious process; they show no signs of complacency or concession, despite the fatigue and ill-health that are referred to with increasing frequency in the painter's letters. And there was no repose: depending on the weather, Cézanne would either hire the services of a driver and have himself taken by coach to distant subjects, or would go on foot to those nearer by. 'It is none the less painful to have to realize', he wrote, 'that

past, and in so doing validates the theories, which themselves are always easy; it is only proving what one believes that presents serious obstacles. So I am carrying on with my research; but I've just re-read your letter and I realize that my answers are always beside the point. You must forgive me – the reason is, as I told

52 *Ibid.*, p.326.
53. *Ibid.*, p.276.
54. Bernard, *Conversations avec Cézanne* (see n. 39), p.24.

the improvement which manifests itself in the comprehension of nature, as regards the form of the painting and the development of the means of expression, should be accompanied by old age and a weakening of the body.'[55] His last letters are tinged with a certain melancholy caused by a feeling that poor health might prevent him from realizing the 'dream of art' he had been pursuing all his life. The belated renown achieved by his work did nothing to convince Cézanne that he had reached his goal.[56] He never admitted to any achievement without underlining the painful slowness of his progress.

But since he had sworn to 'die painting, rather than descend into degrading senility', he worked every day, even during the last year of his life, defying the sweltering heat of the summer of 1906, occasionally taking refuge in the slightly cooler air around the banks of the Arc near the Trois Sautets bridge. 'Here', he wrote, 'on the river-bank, there are myriad subjects; the same view seen from different angles offers a powerfully interesting subject for study, and so varied that I think I could occupy myself for months without changing places, simply by leaning slightly to the right or the left.'[57] That he no longer felt the need to move from one site to another indicates that Cézanne had developed a perception of incredible acuity, able to capture the smallest variations of light and colour. This was a source of considerable satisfaction to him, and the results of his studies in this area are embodied in a series of subtle and highly complex water-colours. It was in this medium, which permits no second thoughts, that he achieved to its fullest the sureness of stroke he so tirelessly sought.

By September, his letters to his son were full of anxiety: 'I am in such a state with mental problems . . . I see everything quite black . . . I regret enormously the state of nervousness in which I find myself . . . Nervous system much enfeebled, only oil painting can sustain me. I must carry on.' Then, October's longed-for cooler weather and a sudden autumn storm proved fatal. Caught out-of-doors, wrote his sister Marie, ' . . . he stayed out in the rain for several hours on Monday; he was brought back on a laundry cart and two men carried him to his room. At first light the following day he went into the garden [of the Lauves studio] to work on the portrait of Vallier under the Linden tree; when he came back, he was in a state of collapse.'[58] Cézanne died a few days later, on 23 October, in his lodgings on the rue Boulegon.

---

55. Cézanne, *Correspondance*, p.313.
56. In 1906, ten of his paintings were shown at the Salon d'Automne. This institution, which was founded in 1903 to show the most advanced painting trends, exhibited thirty-three works by Cézanne in 1904, and Roger Marx published a highly favourable review of this presentation in the *Gazette des beaux-arts*.
57. Cézanne, *Correspondance*, p.324.
58. *Ibid.*, letter from Marie Cézanne to her nephew Paul, p.333.

THE PLATES

Head of an Old Man, c.1865

51 × 48cm, Musée d'Orsay, Paris

The exact identity of the model for this work is not known. It represents one of Cézanne's first portraits and was almost certainly executed in Paris. The artist painted the old man's head over another, unfinished work, which featured a procession of penitents that can still be glimpsed in the lower right-hand corner of the canvas. The portrait, which also remains unfinished, is notable for the decisive execution and strong relief characteristic of this early period, when Cézanne was striving to find a personal style somewhere between Courbet, whose works he had become familiar with since his arrival in Paris in 1861, and Manet, whose *Déjeuner sur l'herbe*, exhibited at the Salon des Refusés in 1863, he greatly admired.

The marked convexity of the skull has been achieved through a series of heavy, distinct strokes that reinforce the highly structured quality of the image. The volume is created by the strong contrast between the areas of light and dark, which are juxtaposed without any intermediary shading. The paint has been applied with a brush, resulting in a delicacy of treatment that was to be abandoned the following year, in favour of the more compact palette-knife stroke used for the series of portraits executed in 1866 (*Uncle Dominique*).

WHAT WOULD YOU DO IF YOU WON A POOLS FORTUNE?

Still Life with Sugar Pot, Pears and Blue Cup, c.1866

30 × 41cm, Musée d'Orsay, Paris

Executed in less conventional manner than the earlier *Still Life with Bread and Eggs* (Cincinnati Art Museum), which is signed and dated 1865, this small painting embodies Cézanne's new style. It can be perceived as a manifesto, announcing the new direction that the painter's work was to take. The force of the almost Expressionist handling links it to the 'constructed' portraits from the same year.

In spite of its traditional dark ground, which limits the pictorial depth and forces the portrayed objects into the foreground, and in spite of the heavy strokes used to convey relief, this picture shows an extremely daring use of colour. There is already a partial building-up of juxtaposed dabs of colour and, even more notable, a use towards the middle of the work of complementary colours to render shade (the green) and light (the red). Instead of employing shading, the artist has placed colours from opposite sides of the chromatic circle next to one another.

Still life remained one of Cézanne's preferred themes throughout his career.

This small still life appears in the large painting executed the same year (see p. 7) that depicts the artist's father reading the newspaper called *L'Evénement* (National Gallery, Washington). This 'painting-within-a-painting' device adds an autobiographical element to the portrait that is not immediately evident. First of all, the link between the still life and the image of his father suggests an acceptance of the painter's new orientation, or at least of his choice of profession. The link with *L'Evénement*, on the other hand, in which Cézanne's friend Zola had recently published a vigorous defence of Manet, represents an appeal to the critic, who had hitherto written nothing positive about Cézanne. As his father was not a regular reader of *L'Evénement*, but subscribed to another Republican newspaper, *Le Siècle*, the association of the still life and the newspaper within the same painting was clearly a deliberate gesture on Cézanne's part. Moreover, an X-ray examination of the painting has revealed that the title of the newspaper was originally given as *Le Siècle*. Cézanne evidently altered the name after the painting was begun, probably following the publication of Zola's articles.

The Negro Scipion, c.1867

107 × 83cm, Museo de Arte, São Paulo

This painting, which was probably executed in Paris in 1867, belonged for many years to Monet, who described it enthusiastically as 'a piece of great power'. Scipion was a model at the Académie Suisse, where Cézanne worked frequently following his arrival in Paris. This work is one of the very few from the period painted after a live model. Cézanne devoted much of his time to drawing, and the compositions of many of his paintings were based on studies taken from his sketchbooks, which he filled not only at the Académie Suisse, but also during long sessions spent in the sculpture collection at the Louvre.

The simplicity and solidity of this work, together with the finely achieved rendering of the musculature, make it a highly successful exercise in realism. The black outlines, delicately highlighted in red, recall Daumier. The large, bright area on the right (presumably a piece of drapery), which serves both as arm-rest and ground, reinforces by its almost abstract flatness the 'realness' of the hand. One of the picture's most surprising features is the freedom of the brushstrokes representing the trousers: these strokes seem arbitrary – again, almost abstract – for they mirror neither the volume of the leg nor the folds of the material. They represent a purely pictorial element within a representational work, as does the broad brushstroke that runs alongside the left hand, emphasizing its length and setting it off from the background.

Winding Road in Provence, c.1868

91 × 71cm, Montreal Museum of Fine Arts

Cézanne painted very few landscapes before 1872, and nearly all of them were executed in his native Provence, where he regularly spent his summer holidays. This quickly painted, possibly even unfinished picture, in generally rather dark tones, obviously relates to the work of the Barbizon painters. It also provides clear proof of the crucial importance of Cézanne's subsequent stay in Pontoise (1872–4) and the advice he received from Pissarro. The work nevertheless represents one of Cézanne's first attempts to confront directly the subject within the context of nature, at a period when he had not yet gained sufficient confidence to break away from the narrative painting that allowed him to give free rein to his fantasies and to channel his latent violence (see *The Rape, c.*1867, *The Murder, c.*1867–8, and *The Temptation of St Anthony, c.*1870 [p. 55]).

This painting is the first in a series that the artist continued in Auvers (p.59) and that he took up again in the final years of his career. In these works, Cézanne frequently depicted views featuring a bend in a road – a manifestation of his interest in effects of spatial depth and perspective (Reff, 1989). Here, the horizon, which is largely filled by an extensive area of green (the mountain) evidently painted at the last moment to cover the black ground, acts as a screen that prevents the road from receding into the distance and brings all the elements of the landscape back to the two-dimensional surface of the canvas. As a result, the curved road is perceived as a vertical form rather than a perspective view of parallel lines. In a letter written to his friend Numa Coste towards the end of November 1868, Cézanne makes reference to a landscape that may well have been this one: 'I am still working very hard on a landscape of a view near the Arc; it's still for the Salon, possibly the 1869 one?' (Cézanne, *Correspondance*, p.134). The dating of the letter coincides with the autumnally rust-coloured areas in the lower right. Cézanne's remark also indicates a certain change of heart regarding the landscape genre: he now considered it important enough to merit exhibition at the Salon. Moreover, his Café Guerbois friends, Pissarro and Monet, had recently succeeded in being accepted by the Salon jury, the former with several views of Pontoise and the latter with a view of Le Havre.

Paul Alexis Reading to Émile Zola, c.1869–70

130 × 160cm, Museo de Arte, São Paulo

This unfinished work, which was found in the attic of Zola's house in Médan a number of years after his death, appears at first to be simply an anecdotal scene of the writer's daily life at his Paris home on the rue de la Condamine. On a more covert level, however, it represents a tribute to Manet, whom Zola had so brilliantly defended and whom at this period Cézanne still admired. The framing of the composition, the static pose of the figures and the relatively shallow pictorial space recall the monumental works executed in 1868 by the leader of the Batignolles group (*Déjeuner dans l'atelier*, *Le Balcon*, both accepted by the Salon jury in 1869). Even in choosing to do this intimate portrait of his friend (the only one in existence, as far as we know), Cézanne was undoubtedly influenced by Manet; for Manet painted portraits of a number of critics, including Astruc (1864), Duret (1888) and Zola himself (accepted by the Salon in 1868), whom he depicted surrounded by an array of artistic and literary references.

In this work, Zola's summarily sketched-in garment draws the viewer's attention to the expression on his face, intent and concentrated as he listens to the voice of his friend Paul Alexis. Alexis was a journalist and naturalist novelist, a native like Cézanne of Aix-en-Provence, whom the painter had introduced into Zola's circle in 1869. His presence here transforms the painting into a manifesto of realism – a realism to which Cézanne himself aspired, but which he had not yet succeeded in translating into a personal style. Owing both to its quick and sketchy rendering and the patch of light it introduces into the left-hand side of the painting, the sheet of paper held by Alexis represents a pictorial element with a new status: anticipating 'pure' painting, it allows us a glimpse of the enormous potential contained in a few brief brushstrokes.

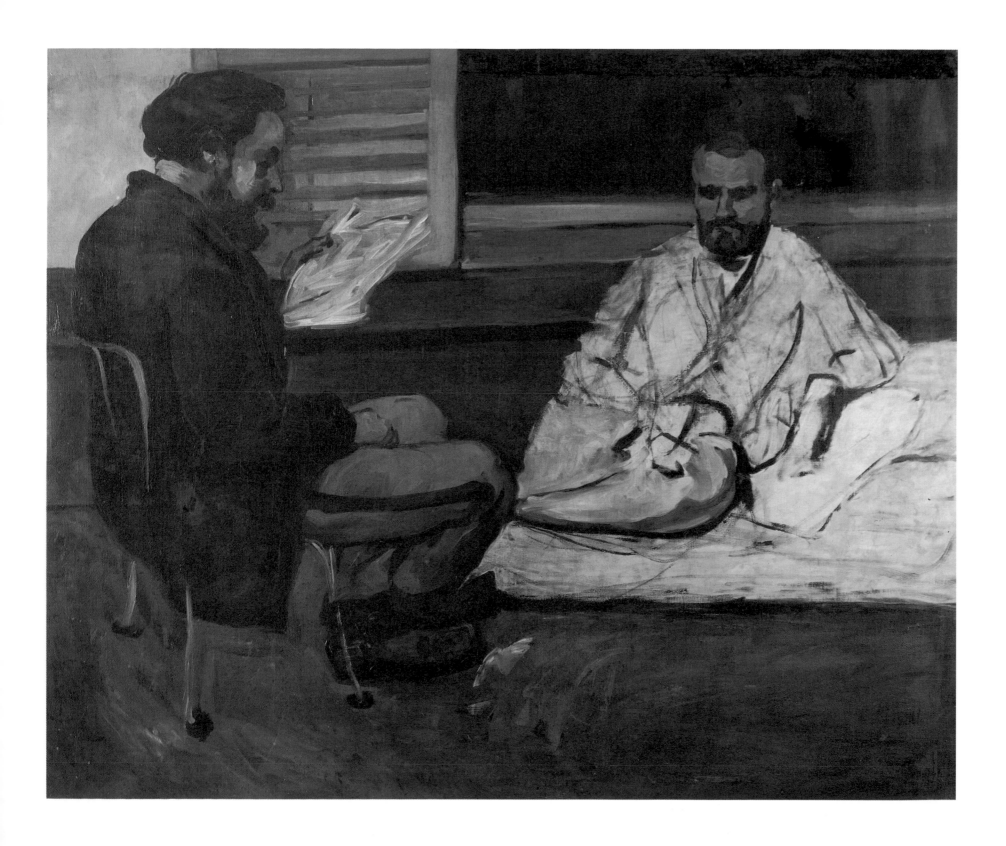

The Temptation of St Anthony, c.1870

54 × 73cm, Fondation Collection E.G. Bührle, Zurich

In spite of the fact that it treats of a theme represented often within the Western artistic tradition, this work remains enigmatic. It deals with the same subject and bears the same title as a novel by Flaubert published in serialized form in the magazine *L'Artiste* from 1856 to 1857. Both sombre and sensual, 'troubling, verging on the hallucinatory' (Fry), the painting offers a glimpse of the inner world that is clearly revealed by the young Cézanne's correspondence with Zola. Responding to the evident differences that separate the work from more usual iconographical renderings, most analysts look for hidden biographical elements, which they each then proceed to decode according to different approaches in interpretation. References are made to the artist's private life (his affair with Hortense Fiquet), to the literature of the period (Flaubert, Baudelaire, Zola), to his sketchbooks (for the pose of the figures) and to psychoanalysis. Almost all agree, however, that the work represents a highly personal and conflict-ridden vision of man's relationship to woman, in which desire and guilt are at odds.

This painting is often linked to two others from the same period, executed in the same dark tones and also considered to be autobiographical: *Le Déjeuner sur l'herbe* (private collection) and *Pastoral (Idyll)* (Musée d'Orsay, Paris). Whatever the underlying meaning of this group of works, it is the fruit of a still fundamentally narrative approach to painting. Cézanne was deliberately choosing to express the inner world of his fantasies rather than coming to grips with the pictorial object. Monet actually described Cézanne as 'the Flaubert of painting, a bit heavy, stubborn, painstaking, furiously chasing after a solid rhythm of forms and of colours, often achieving it, sometimes getting bogged down in the gropings of a genius struggling pathetically to find himself' (Adriani, 1981, p. 9, note 1).

Formally speaking, this painting is the original well-spring of the long series of *Bathers* that Cézanne worked on throughout his life. The positions of the figures, their triangular arrangement and their concentration into isolated groups across the canvas are all elements that were to reappear year after year, independent of the gradual lightening of the palette and the development of the brushstroke.

Landscape with a Watermill, c.1871

41 × 54cm, Yale University Art Gallery, New Haven

This landscape, a truly transitional work, was probably painted during Cézanne's stay in Provence at the time of the Franco-Prussian War. There is a possibility, however, that it is one of the earliest of the outdoor studies painted in the company of Pissarro the following year, in the area surrounding Pontoise. Whatever the case, Cézanne seems to have temporarily set aside his rather juvenile desire for disapproval in order to develop his powers of observing nature, which he renders here with a far more confident and controlled stroke. The details of the landscape tend to disappear, making way for a composition of areas of light colour out of which emerges a delicate, indefinite image. The texture of the paint surface and the tones employed related the work to another entitled *The House of the Hanged Man*, which was exhibited at Nadar's studio in 1874 during the first exhibition of the Société anonyme des artistes peintres, sculpteurs, graveurs, etc. – an event referred to by critics of the period as an 'Impressionist' exhibition.

Road at Auvers-sur-Oise, c.1873–4

55.2 × 46.2cm, National Gallery of Canada, Ottawa

Pissarro had gathered around him in Pontoise a small group of friends who shared an interest in painting outdoors. Guillaumin made several short stays there between his various jobs for the Highways Department; and Béliard, another habitué of the Café Guerbois, visited occasionally in search of subjects. In the spring of 1872, Cézanne also made the trip. Under the influence of Pissarro, he began consistently selecting subjects from nature, and he travelled continually around the Pontoise and Auvers regions in search of suitable sites. The little village of Auvers, with its thatched roofs and unpaved roads, was an ideal source of one of his favourite themes: the winding road. By September 1872, Pissarro was announcing proudly to Guillemet: 'Our friend Cézanne gives much cause for hope and I have seen – and actually have at home – a painting of a vigour and force that are quite remarkable. If, as I hope, he stays some time in Auvers, where he is going to live, he will surprise many artists who passed judgement on him rather too quickly.' (Quoted by John Rewald, *Cézanne, sa vie, son, oeuvre, son amitié pour Zola*, 1939, p. 196.)

This study, executed on a dull day, illustrates clearly the positive effects of Pissarro's advice concerning the use of a brighter palette based on the three complementary colours and the application of a thin print layer using small strokes. Cézanne lightened his colour range by gradually abandoning the use of black and of heavy outlines. Unlike the 'Impressionists', however, he did not employ light to decompose forms: painting out of doors did not, for him, mean relinquishing his search for the formal balance he saw as essential to the integrity of a painting. Even though the composition is to some extent imposed by the subject, it is still the painter's role to frame the work, and to portray the atmospheric layers and the infinitely varying play of light. Another characteristic that distinguished him from the Impressionists was the relative slowness with which he worked. This quality is made evident here in the meticulous application of the green strokes, highlighted in yellow, that run along the edges of the road, and again in the veritable mosaic of many-coloured strokes that are used to 'build' the road, both in height and depth.

A Modern Olympia, 1873

46 × 55cm, Musée d'Orsay, Paris

Cézanne presented this painting at the Première Exposition de la Société anonyme des artistes peintres, sculpteurs, graveurs, etc., which opened at Nadar's studio on 15 April 1874. The accompanying catalogue stated the owner as being Dr Gachet, a supporter of new painting of some years' standing who had recently acquired a house in Auvers. Interestingly, the title of the work appears in the catalogue followed by the word 'Sketch'.

The extremely free handling and evident speed of execution were achieved in spite of the fact that the theme had already been treated by Cézanne in almost precisely the same terms – although in darker tones – some years before (*A Modern Olympia [The Pasha]*, *c.*1869–70). The painting is, moreover, a reinterpretation of Manet's *Olympia* (1863). Following Pissarro's advice and using, here, a markedly lighter palette, Cézanne was perhaps hoping that this canvas would achieve in 1874 the same rather scandalous success won by Manet's version at the Salon of 1865.

But the critics of the period refused to be drawn: Manet's harsh realism was, they felt, far more striking. The overall impact of this composition, which features Cézanne himself as the spectator of his own fantasy, has its roots too obviously in dreams to be genuinely shocking. This, at least, was the view expressed by Marc de Montifaud (actually the pseudonym of a woman, Marie-Emilie Chartroule de Montifaud) in a review of the Boulevard de Capucines exhibition:

> . . . The Sunday public saw fit to laugh at the fantastic figure appearing to an opium smoker, suspended in a drug-laden haze. This apparition of pink and naked flesh – thrust forward by some kind of demon through the cloudy heavens, out of which is created, like a voluptuous vision, a zone of artificial paradise – has, it must be admitted, left even the most stalwart quite breathless; Mr Cézanne appears to be nothing less than some kind of madman, shaken as he paints by fits of *delirium tremens*. People have refused to see this Baudelaire-inspired creation as a dream arising out of oriental mists, which could only be rendered in the strange language of the imaginary. Is not incoherence the very nature, a characteristic feature of wholesome sleep? Why look for an indecent joke, a source of scandal in the *Olympia*? It is actually nothing more than one of the more extravagant of the hashish-based images that emerge from the host of ribald dreams that must still linger in the corridors of the Hôtel Pimodan . . . (*L'Artiste*, 1 May 1874, p. 310.)

In spite of the over-charged setting of the courtesan's world, in which the anecdotal still takes precedence over the compositional, this painting nevertheless shows signs of an attempt to break down and re-order perspectival space – an undertaking that was to become one of the central features of Cézanne's work.

Three Bathers, c.1875–7

19 × 22cm, Musée d'Orsay, Paris

The bathers theme recurred in Cézanne's work regularly during the mid-1870s, representing for him an opportunity to reestablish his links with the old masters. Prior to this, he had shown an occasional interest in the subject in his sketchbooks and also in several 'lunch on the grass' scenes, which often conceal a complex personal symbolism similar to that found in *The Temptation of St Anthony* (p. 55). One suggested source of the bathing theme is a small ink drawing that appears on the back of a letter sent to Zola in 1859; this sketch, which depicts three young bathers beneath a tree (almost certainly the artist, Baille and Zola), conjures up the pleasant days the artist spent with his friends in the countryside surrounding Aix.

Here, the triangular composition of the female figures, whose highly studied, classical poses are clearly inspired by early Italian and French engravings, are evidence of the painter's desire to work within a certain tradition. The parallels drawn by Krumrine between this painting and two preparatory works – a drawing and a water-colour – enable us to perceive a fourth figure, whose head alone appears and whom the seated figure seems to be pushing back (Krumrine, 1989 [exhib. cat.]). These iconographical details, together with the evasive movement sketched by the central figure, encourage us to see in this work a subtle re-appearance of the spectator/voyeur of the *Modern Olympia* (p. 61). It is hard to know if this is simply chance, a lingering echo of the artist's fantasy, or a prelude to the more explicit eroticism of a painting from 1880, entitled *La lutte d'amour*, which was apparently the final expression of Cézanne's taste for scenes full of sexual violence and literary allusion.

Because of its small size, the summary handling of the landscape and of the figures' modelling, and its generally unfinished look, this canvas can be classified as one of the many 'studies' on the bathers theme. It was not until the end of his life (see p. 123) that Cézanne arrived at definitive solutions to the difficult problems posed by integrating the nude figure into a natural setting. The paintings known as *The Large Bathers* are the masterly culmination of this endeavour.

Plate of Apples, c.1877

46 × 55cm, Art Institute, Chicago

'I want to astonish Paris with an apple,' (reported by Gustave Geffroy, *Monet* [Paris: Macula, 1980], p. 328). This example of southern wit, uttered by Cézanne in 1894 during a friendly gathering at Monet's house, in Giverny, that was also attended by Geffroy, Mirbeau, Rodin and Clemenceau, is very revealing of his attitude to painting. He hated everything that was exhibited at what he called 'Bouguereau's Salon', and all his life he sought a personal style capable of imbuing the most humble objects with nobility.

This *Plate of Apples* shows clearly just how far, by 1877, Cézanne had moved away from the Impressionists, despite having recently participated in their Third Exhibition. He had evidently learned a great deal from Pissarro's instruction and has achieved a masterly control of colour and its brilliance that went far beyond anything he had done before. What is most striking about this particular painting, however, is its link with the work of Chardin, which Cézanne had been studying at the Louvre since the end of the 1860s.

Cézanne was searching for a 'formula' that would enable him to convey a feeling of volume without resorting to the conventional device of chiaroscuro, which creates an effect of relief, or 'modelling', through the gradual shading of a single colour. Cézanne's major technical innovation centered on his creation of this effect through a use of different colours, of varying degrees of luminosity, applied side by side in small, slightly overlapping strokes. When speaking of his own technique, he preferred to use the word 'modulating' rather than 'modelling'.

Cézanne's other main concern in his approach to still life was to unify the pictorial space and thus avoid a static effect that would contradict the mobility of the colours. Here, this unification is obtained by the circular movement created by the repetition of blue decorative pattern, which starts in the back and moves through to the foreground, echoing the circular shape of the dish. The work's high-angle viewpoint permits the painter to raise slightly the corner of the table near the centre, which destabilizes it in relation to the picture plane and contributes to the overall spatial movement. This device also has the effect of eliminating depth and emphasizing the volume of the fruit.

There are five known still lifes that have this ochre-coloured wallpaper with blue designs as a ground, and the decorative motif also appears in the background of a portrait of the artist's wife (p. 67), dating from 1877. It seems likely that these canvases were executed in the same Paris apartment, probably the one at 67 rue de l'Ouest. All the works in the group show the same concentrated attempt to protect the volumes from the decomposing effects of light, but it is in *Plate of Apples* that the artist achieves his goal most completely.

Madame Cézanne in a Red Armchair, c.1877

72.5 × 56cm, Museum of Fine Arts, Boston

Through the richness and density of its coloured surface and the glowing luminosity it seems to emit, this canvas provides proof of Cézanne's newly acquired skill and assurance following his 'passage' through Impressionism. Turning his back on the ephemeral, he endeavoured, for a time, to create stable forms. His aim is made abundantly clear by the overall effect of this composition. It is through an exhaustive analysis of colour and its potential for constructing space that the artist has succeeded in endowing this figure with its quite extraordinary monumentality.

The subject of the work occupies all the space in the picture and is set in a frame that cuts off certain parts of the image (the armchair runs over the edge of the canvas). The figure barely stands out against the chair, the chair barely against the background; the spaces between the various elements are almost imperceptible, and there are virtually no shadows. The carefully articulated planes of the left half of the painting break down entirely on the right. A very obvious alteration running along the bent arm and the unfinished area of the skirt are evidence of the problems of integration Cézanne was still facing when it came to moving from plane to volume. An overall unity is nevertheless achieved through a masterly distribution of blues and greens across the surface of the picture.

The many portraits of his wife, Hortense Fiquet, painted throughout Cézanne's career show that he preferred her as a model above all others. She sat for him until 1895. After that, she spent most of her time in Paris and the artist, who remained in Aix, was obliged to turn to others in his immediate circle, such as his gardener and local farm workers. The seemingly endless sittings required for every portrait must have demanded similarly endless patience on the part of anyone who agreed to pose.

The Bridge at Maincy, c.1879–80

58 × 72cm, Musée d'Orsay, Paris

Since his stay in Pontoise with Pissarro, Cézanne had taken to regularly touring the area surrounding Paris in search of subjects. Having been once again refused by the Salon in 1879, he settled for a few months in Melun. To the east, in the little village of Maincy, near Vaux-le-Vicomte, he discovered the bridge depicted here, which crosses the Almont and links the hamlet of Trois-Moulins to the village. Cézanne chose to isolate the bridge in a frontal view, giving only the vaguest intimation of the mill buildings on the left, which lends the landscape a distinct feeling of solidity.

The image of a calm stretch of water reflecting elements of a landscape was a subject much favoured by the Impressionists. Cézanne approaches it here in a typically personal fashion, making no attempt to render atmosphere or capture the fleeting quality of light. Using a technique that was to become characteristic of him – strokes that are either square or applied in a system of parallel hatchings, both very visible and employed here almost literally to 'construct' the bridge, its reflection and the tangle of branches – he presents us with an image built up from innumerable, light-catching facets.

Like so many of Cézanne's 'pure' landscapes, from which all human presence is rigorously excluded, this solid, balanced landscape seems to be a place of great stillness. The spectator is none the less encouraged to scan the unmoving surface by a dab of white near the centre. The function of this apparently random stroke is to instil the predominating green with movement and to force the eye to travel from one bank to the other, never going beyond the bridge, but remaining within the boundaries set by the points of light scattered across the painting.

Médan, the Castle, c.1879–81

59 × 72cm, Museums and Art Galleries, Glasgow

In 1878, Zola had bought a country house at Médan, on the Seine. Its red shutters and its chimneys can be spotted in this painting to the right, between two poplars. Cézanne spent several holidays there. The master of the house soon began to gather around him friends and members of the 'naturalist' group, and Cézanne – his childhood friend – was always warmly welcomed among them.

The invitation to visit received in the autumn of 1879 gave particular pleasure to Cézanne, ' . . . especially at this period', he wrote, 'when the countryside is really stunning. – It seems as if the silence is greater' (letter dated 27 September 1879).

As is the case for most of Cézanne's paintings, the majority of which are not dated, it is difficult to link this work to a particular visit. The spot from which it was painted is, however, clearly identifiable. Zola owned a small island in the Seine, opposite his property, that was accessible by boat; to do this painting Cézanne obviously set up his easel on the island. The river-banks are rendered by the technique characteristic of this period: juxtaposed parallel strokes applied diagonally. It is a technique that was also employed for a time by Gauguin, who owned this painting for a number of years. This helps us to understand what lay behind Cézanne's complaint that Gauguin had 'stolen his little sensation'.

Self-portrait, c.1880

33 × 26cm, National Gallery, London

Cézanne's various portraits have often been criticized for their emphasis on formal analysis at the expense of insight into the individual psychology of the model. The same reproach cannot be made of his self-portraits, which rival those of Rembrandt in number and importance. Coming back periodically to his own face was probably a form of stocktaking. Generally speaking, as he scrutinized himself in the mirror, the artist did little to hide his state of mind, and as a result each image allows us to discern something of his disposition. Here, the gentle gaze and the slightly amused look are in striking contrast to the anxiety, dissatisfaction and even anger apparent in self-portraits from previous years. An example of these less tranquil images is the one in which a landscape by Guillaumin appears in the background (Musée d'Orsay, Paris).

Despite the impatience expressed in his letters at his slow rate of progress, Cézanne seems to have achieved a certain serenity of mind during these years spent in the north, in regular contact with his closest friends – Pissarro, whom he visited again in Pontoise, and Zola in Médan. The emphasis in this work on clear, parallel brushstrokes and the subtle re-use in the foreground of a grey tone from the rear are evidence, moreover, of a new artistic confidence.

The wallpaper with a diamond-shaped pattern to be seen here in the background, which also appears in several still lifes, seems to indicate a date just prior to his departure for Melun or shortly after his return to Paris, in the spring of 1880. If this is the case, the painting must have been executed in the apartment located at 32 rue de l'Ouest (letter to Zola dated 10 May 1880).

Apples and Plate of Biscuits, c.1879–82

46 × 55cm, Musée de l'Orangerie, Paris

Here again, the background – blue wallpaper covered with a delicate leaf pattern – enables us to give an approximate date to the painting, for it reappears in a number of other works from the same period (eleven still lifes, according to Venturi's catalogue), including the *Portrait of Louis Guillaume* (National Gallery, Washington). This still life was almost certainly executed in one of the various Paris apartments inhabited by Cézanne during these years.

The work is unusual in the extreme simplicity of its composition: we are shown a selection of fruit and a plate placed next to each other on a sideboard. The spareness of the painting's structure conveys an impression that the central plane bearing the fruit is in a state of virtual 'levitation' in relation to the other planes – the front of the sideboard and the blue papered background – which are exactly parallel to the picture plane, thus accentuating its frontality. And the tilted angle of the biscuit plate further reinforces the flatness of the support.

In his rendering of the relief of the apples, the artist, with enormous skill, creates the impression of a slight recession in the space of the plane represented by the top of the sideboard. It is this that leads the viewer into the perception of the 'step-like' articulation of the three planes and guarantees the spatial mobility of the painting. In this open and rhythmic space, the fruit's 'richness of colour' can 'expand to its fullest' (Cézanne).

The work's extremely close-up viewpoint enables the artist to concentrate on one of the fundamental problems posed by still life: the unification of disparate elements so that the overall effect is not one of content (object) and container (space). Here, unity is achieved through the delicacy with which the parallel brushstrokes are applied over the whole surface and through the discreet reappearance in the front of the background colour.

Houses in Provence (Vicinity of L'Estaque), c.1879–82

65 × 81cm, National Gallery of Art, Washington

On his return to Provence in the winter of 1882, Cézanne continued to use the parallel, diagonally applied brushstroke perfected during the Île de France period. Here, we see an unusually rigorous and exhaustive application of this technique designed to unite the pictorial surface. The approach was gradually to be abandoned, however, in favour of less uniform strokes whose variety enabled the artist to render both volumes and successive spatial planes.

By giving the same texture to the whole of the painting's surface and distributing the tonal values equally across the landscape, Cézanne was straying further than ever from the traditional techniques of representation. The light is rhythmically diffused through a myriad of small brushstrokes, which has the effect of underlining the constructive function of the stroke itself in the creation of the image. Here, Cézanne appears clearly as a forerunner of Seurat.

The Sea at L'Estaque, c.1883

73 × 92cm, Musée du Louvre, Paris

In May 1883, Cézanne wrote to inform his friend Zola that he had 'rented a little house with a garden at L'Estaque, just above the station, at the foot of the hill, where behind me rise the rocks and the pines'. These majestic pines serve as the frame for this view of the village, in which the vastly simplified houses are reduced to the role of providing the composition with geometric shapes and coloured planes.

In spite of the frame of trees and the strong foreground element represented by the promontory, the sea is not perceived as a plane receding into the distance, but as a solid plane parallel to the pictorial surface. The luminosity of this plane is practically uniform and corresponds to that of the similarly coloured patches that appear in the foreground (the block on the left-hand side, for example), which has the effect of bringing the horizon forward.

Still Life with Chest, c.1882–7

71 × 90cm, Neue Pinakothek, Munich

This very 'classical' composition, depicting ordinary everyday objects, stands out against a rigorously planimetric background formed by a chest of drawers and a screen, whose rococo pattern contrasts pleasingly with the overall severity of the image. The balance of the whole is extremely subtle.

The 'sculptural' effect of the pleats in the pushed-up tablecloth is quite striking: it is as if the folds might subside at any moment were it not for the solidity instilled in them by the artist. As well as serving to counterbalance the green jar and the sugar bowl, they draw attention to the fragility of the whole arrangement. At first glance, the table seems to obey the rules of perspective. In fact, however, it is divided into two sections: the straight line representing its front edge is broken towards the middle, beneath the plate of apples, as if it were being seen from the two different points of view. The cloth serves to unite the table top, thus reducing a visual tension that might otherwise have destroyed the integrity of the image.

View of L'Estaque and the Château d'If, c.1882–5

73 × 60cm, Fitzwilliam Museum, Cambridge

The view of the bay of Marseilles from the village of L'Estaque was for several years one of Cézanne's most 'explored' motifs. He knew the area well, for he had taken refuge there during the Franco-Prussian War, staying in a house owned by his mother. He worked there again in 1876, and then settled in the village in 1878 so as to be able to travel alternatively to Marseilles, to visit Hortense and his son Paul, and to Aix, to see his parents, who were still not aware of his family's existence.

Cézanne noted the very special character of this landcape in 1876. In his desire to render nature faithfully without employing the traditional techniques of modelling, he discovered the necessary means of expression 'on the spot', as it were, as the result of a careful observation of the subject itself. As he wrote to Pissarro:

> I have started two little subjects where there is the sea . . . It's like a playing card. Red roofs against the blue sea. If the weather is favourable, perhaps I might follow them through to the end . . . But there are subjects that would require three or four months work, which would be possible, for the vegetation doesn't change. It's olive trees and pines, which always keep their leaves. The sun is so appalling that it seems as though objects are silhouetted not only in black and white, but in blue, red, brown and violet. I may be mistaken, but it seems to me the very opposite of modelling. (Cézanne, *Correspondance*, p. 152.)

This is a transitional work, situated between *Médan, the Castle*, to which it is closely related, and the famous views entitled *Gulf of Marseilles* (Metropolitan Museum of Art, New York; Art Institute, Chicago), which are simultaneously more dense and less detailed. The painting actually represents a very important stage in Cézanne's development, for it was while working on this subject that he succeeded in arriving at a structure in which spatial depth is obtained exclusively through the contrasting of warm and cold colours.

House and Farm at the Jas de Bouffan, c.1885

60.5 × 73.5cm, Narodnie Galerie, Prague

This picture is the most complete of the many views of the family home painted by Cézanne during the periods when he withdrew there from Paris.

The systematic use of the parallel hatched stroke (see p. 77) has been almost entirely replaced by a more uniform handling of a noticeably thinner paint layer, which seems at first glance to be tending towards a certain representational realism. However, the painter stops his description of the site when it is only partially complete, and concentrates instead on the composition of planes within a two-dimensional space that allowed for no perspectival vistas.

Like the view of Gardanne painted at around the same time, this work shows clearly that Cézanne has not lost contact with his starting-point in the physical world. But since the image is an abstract reconstruction of that world, a 'harmony parallel to nature', as he wrote to Émile Bernard, the painter is free to compose on a single pictorial surface horizontal bands rising one above the other, a main building that is entirely flat, and a farmhouse whose planes fit rather oddly into one another, creating a faint impression of depth. It is works such as this one that were the source, in 1908, of Braque's first Cubist investigations.

The Blue Vase, c.1883–7

61 × 50cm, Musée d'Orsay, Paris

During his stay in Auvers, Cézanne made a number of paintings of flowers, which Madame Gachet would arrange for him in vases (e.g. *Delft Vase with Dahlias* 1873, Louvre, Paris). In the years that followed, he often chose to represent flowers and fruit together, in the same composition. Although the objects in a still life are pre-arranged, the successful completion of such a composition is not necessarily any easier, and the slowness with which Cézanne worked frequently forced him into abandoning a subject when the flowers wilted. He even resorted, on occasion, to using artificial ones.

This unfinished canvas allows us a few glimpses of the flowing lines of the preparatory sketch, the simple and summary positioning of objects that served as an initial compositional guide. It also shows examples of the open and barely perceptible outlines that would recur often in the great still lifes of the 1890s.

The chromatic harmony of this painting, which glows almost like a pastel, is truly remarkable. The overall unity of the work is achieved through a delicate echoing of the blues and pinks of the wall in the surface of the table. All the objects possess the same texture – that of the paint itself. The horizontals and verticals give the work a marked stability, which is subtly maintained in a state of precarious equilibrium by the introduction of a diagonal that opens the space up slightly towards the back.

According to the memoirs of Émile Bernard, Cézanne 'meditated paint-brush in hand'. It was surely this faculty that enabled him to capture with such finesse the silent life of objects.

Trees and Houses, c.1885–8

54 × 73cm, Musée de l'Orangerie, Paris

The subject of this painting, which almost certainly depicts a view in the area surrounding the Jas de Bouffan, recalls quite vividly certain canvases by Sisley, Pissarro and Monet. However, Cézanne's planimetric treatment of the view, which combines contrasts of colour and of texture, makes it very different from the creations of his contemporaries.

Through the fineness of the paint layer, the artist has achieved effects of transparency that are normally only obtainable with water-colour. As he wrote to Émile Bernard, '. . . the sensations of colour, which give light, are the reason for the abstractions that prevent me from either covering my canvas or continuing the delimitation of objects when their points of contact are fine and delicate; which is why my image or picture is incomplete' (Cézanne, *Correspondance*, p. 315).

There is a marked contrast in this work between the clarity of the network of curving lines representing the branches and the summary rendering of the houses, which gives priority to space-creating elements at the expense of detail. Both the pink and ochre areas that link the ground and the buildings towards the centre and the extraordinary interpenetration, on the right, of the ochre and the blue of the sky are attempts by the artist to convey the 'sensations of colour' that he mentions to Bernard. The houses do not stand out against a background; they are suspended, caught in the instant of their perception. All the planes interlock on the two-dimensional surface of the support, uniting to create an appearing/disappearing reality to which we can gain access only through the painting of Cézanne.

Mont Sainte-Victoire, c.1886–7

59.6 × 72.5cm, Phillips Collection, Washington

Before 1885 Cézanne only tackled this magnificent subject rather tentatively, concentrating most of his attention on views of L'Estaque and Gardanne. After this date, however, depicting the mountain's unique silhouette and successfully integrating it into pictorial space became a daily challenge. This is one of his earliest efforts, and there exists another almost identical version that is now in the collection of the Courtauld Institute, London. To paint this subject, Cézanne installed his easel at the foot of a huge pine, which not only frames the view (a technique employed similarly at L'Estaque; see pp. 79 and 83), but also provides a sinuous element whose curves and counter-curves echo the profile of the mountain.

It is an extremely soundly constructed work: the various planes rise in tiers one above the other to the summit – a movement that is adroitly prolonged by touches of green – and the plain is integrated smoothly into the base of the mountain. In the light of newly revealed documents, Reff has recently drawn attention to Cézanne's interest in perspective – an interest that this painting confirms (Reff, 1989, pp. 8–15). Within his planimetric composition, the artist has introduced a diagonal (the road) that meets a horizontal (the viaduct) at a vanishing point which, despite being situated outside the painting, nevertheless creates a certain feeling of depth amoing the gently rolling fields. Another vanishing point is situated 'behind' the house on the left, towards which converge the same diagonal represented by the road and another coming from the left. The area enclosed by these two diagonals can be perceived either as receding towards the back of the work or as a vertical form parallel to the picture plane.

This sustained tension between surface and depth, created by the work's various linear and pictorial elements, is a 'classic' instance of the equilibrium characteristic of Cézanne's *oeuvre*.

Mont Sainte-Victoire, c.1885–7

54 × 65cm, Stedelijk Museum, Amsterdam

In contrast to the preceding work, Cézanne here offers the viewer a 'close-up' view of the mountain. The complex spatial ambiguity of the foreground in the previous plate (p. 91) has been eliminated in order to capture completely the breathtaking ascension of the mountain between earth and sky. All the painter's attention is concentrated on the integration of these three elements – earth, sky and mountain – so that together they create a single space, the space of the picture itself. He scrutinizes the mountain's surface, striving to reproduce it in all its chromatic variation.

The great luminosity of this painting emanates from the colours themselves and the skilfully achieved balance between warm and cold values, placed side by side and linked by 'passages' of pure shades. The deliberately restrained brushstrokes, applied in a carefully selected order, provide the only clue to the movement from one plane to another. Cézanne was to develop this technique more systematically over the next ten years (see, p. 111) creating his most spectacular renderings of this particular motif after the turn of the century (see pp. 127, 133 and 135).

Boy in a Red Waistcoat, c.1888–9

80 × 64.5cm, Fondation Collection E.G. Bührle, Zurich

Between 1888 and 1890 Cézanne went back to his old habit of dividing his time between Aix and Paris. During this period, he occupied an apartment on the Quai d'Anjou, and it is probably there that this portrait was painted. Rewald has drawn attention to the frequent recurrence of a number of decorative elements associated with this apartment, including the moulding topped with a wine-coloured strip and the heavily pleated curtain (Rewald, 1984, pp. 174–5). According to Venturi, the boy himself was a young Italian called Michelangelo di Rosa, who worked in Paris at the time as a model (Venturi, 1936, vol. 1, no. 680). There are four other paintings from the period depicting the same boy, seen either in profile or face-on; this three-quarter view is assuredly the most successful.

The model's pose, head supported by hand, was employed by Cézanne several times subsequently, notably in his portraits *Man with a Pipe, Boy with a Skull* and *Italian Girl*. Through its direct allusion to Dürer's famous engraving entitled *Melancholy*, it is almost certainly the pose itself that is the source of the feeling of sadness common to these various figures.

Here, the large arc drawn by the body constitutes the central element of the composition. Firmly anchored in a closed space – blocked off to the left by the diagonal of the curtain, to the rear by the horizontals of the wall and to the right by a triangular area of dark colour – it is echoed by the arc of the arm, which has been deliberately elongated to balance the composition. The arrangement of the remaining planes contributes towards the isolation of the central figure and accentuates the subtly melancholic facial expression.

This painting was shown in Cézanne's first one-man exhibition, held at Vollard's gallery in 1895. Struck by its great restraint and compositional solidity, critic Gustave Geffroy compared the work to the great figure paintings of history.

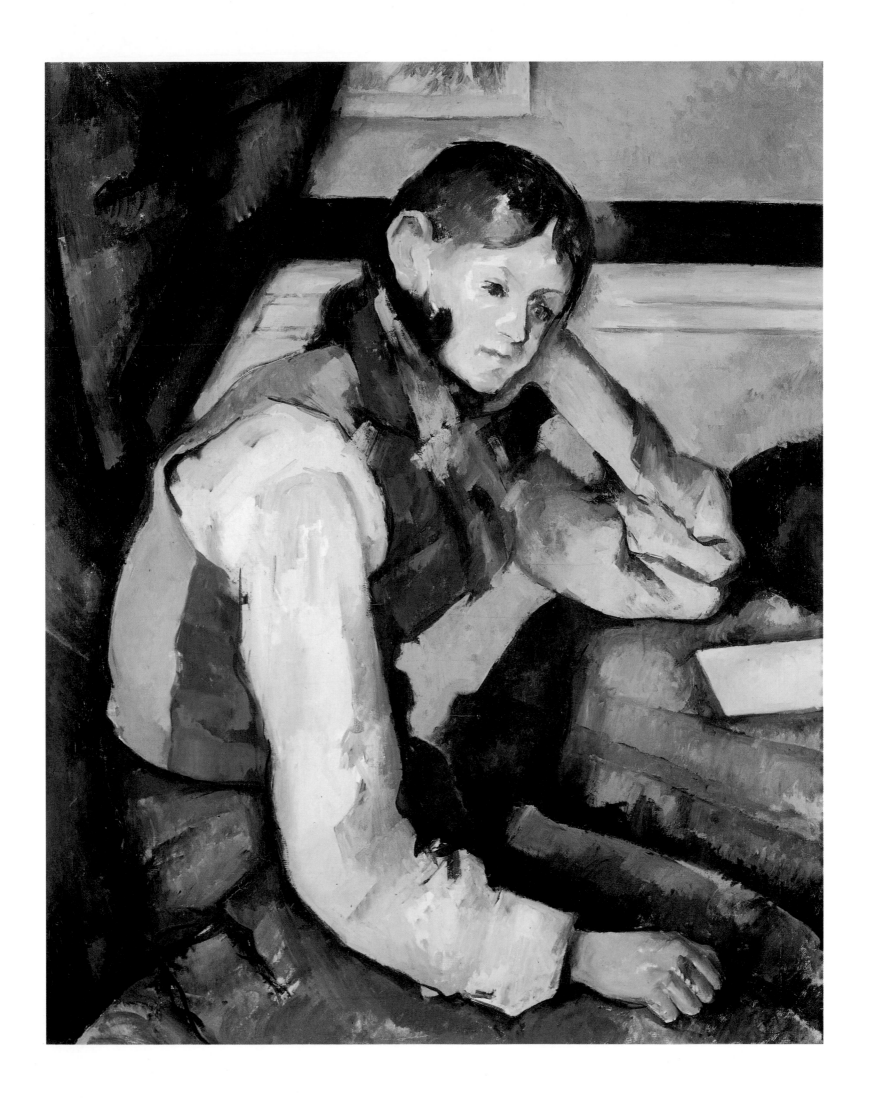

Madame Cézanne in a Red Dress, c.1890–4

116 × 89cm, Metropolitan Museum of Art, New York

If we are to judge by the setting, the canvas reproduced here was painted in the same Paris apartment as the previous one, on the Quai d'Anjou. There exist four versions of this portrait of Madame Cézanne dressed in red and seated in a yellow chair, all of which focus on the artist's investigations concerning the integration of a figure into an enclosed space. In this case, the space is closed off on the right by a piece of heavy drapery, and on the left by a mantelpiece surmounted by a somewhat broader mirror. In order to counteract the symmetry resulting from this framing and avoid an overly static effect, Cézanne has introduced a number of small deviations that combine to create one of the most mobile pictorial spaces of the series and, indeed, of all the portraits painted up to this point.

The artist has inclined the model's torso slightly to the right of the painting's central axis, thus creating a movement that is reinforced by the oval of the arms in the direction of a complete rotation. The entire space is borne along by this centripetal movement, to end up teetering under the impact of the diagonal element introduced into the composition by the strip of moulding and its claret-coloured upper band.

A strong blue tint invades all the tones, creating around the central figure a sort of aerial envelope. Chromatic harmony is achieved through a delicate balance between a limited range of broken colours distributed evenly across the canvas; it is this harmony, moreover, that creates the impression of an area lit by a muted, even light.

Boat and Bathers, c.1890–4

30 × 125cm, Musée de l'Orangerie, Paris

The unusual format of this painting can be attributed to the fact that it was intended as part of a decorative group commissioned by Victor Chocquet for his new house in Paris, where he planned to hang his collection. There exists another panel, entitled *Peacock and Trough*, painted by Cézanne for the same commission. The project as a whole never came to fruition, owing to Chocquet's death in 1891. It seems, however, that in spite of the sad circumstances, the artist completed the painting and sent it to Chocquet's widow, for it appeared in the sale organized after her death in 1899. But while the anecdotal account of the painting's origin is interesting, it must not be allowed to mask its true origin, nor its significance for our understanding of Cézanne.

Painted at a period when Cézanne was working on many studies of isolated groups of bathers, both male and female, this work stands out in every way from the rest of the series, constituting its unique and most complete realization. The recent death of Chocquet, Cézanne's friend and benefactor, is almost certainly behind the reappearance of the boat (which had not been seen since the *Déjeuner sur l'herbe* of 1870), alone in the middle of an infinite space and so evocative of the craft in which Charon ferried his passengers to the Underworld.

What the artist is showing us here is the very antithesis of the world of objectivity. In ambiguous tones, which may be those of either dawn or dusk, the painting bears witness to Cézanne's awareness of his own pure sensation of space. The figures, of indistinguishable sex and painted from memory, are simply forms perfectly integrated into the spaces they inhabit. They are centres of energy, poles between which stretches an infinite calm.

Perhaps Cézanne has succeeded in giving us, through his painting, an image of 'the Open', to which the poet Rainer Maria Rilke alludes in the Eighth Duino Elegy:

With all its eyes the creature sees
'the Open' . . .
. . .
But we, never, not a single day, have we
before us pure space, in which flowers
bloom infinitely. Always it is the world,
and never what is nowhere and unlimited:
the pure, the unwatched, that we breathe,
that we know to be infinite and covet not . . .

Still Life with Peppermint Bottle and Blue Rug, c.1893–5

65 × 81cm, National Gallery of Art, Washington

During the 1890s, the arrangement of the objects depicted in Cézanne's still lifes became even more carefully studied – an expression of his desire to confront fresh pictorial challenges. The skill and evident pleasure with which he altered their position from one canvas to another testify to the importance he accorded to his research into formal innovation.

Having frequently in the past been engrossed by the rendering of the volumetric character of fruit, Cézanne turns here to the transparency of glass and a study of various objects from everyday life: a glass, a water carafe and a bottle of peppermint syrup. What seems at first surprising is the apparently arbitrary complexity of the arrangement; for we are not dealing here with the depiction of a laid table (like the Dutch *Ontbijt*, for example) or the remains of a banquet. On closer examination, however, we see that not a single element could be removed without destroying the work's overall pictorial coherence. It was not Cézanne's goal to create a painting with narrative or allegorical content (as in a traditional still life), but to give to inanimate objects an almost organic logical interconnection.

The heavily-patterned blue carpet (of which Matisse no doubt took note) creates an effective visual contrast with the plain white of the cloth, also animating a section of the pictorial surface and accentuating its opacity. The objects sit, motionless, within a narrow space defined by little more than the hollows of a few folds, surrounded by a truly 'sculptural' form that rises up on the table, obliterating its surface. Near the centre, two pieces of fruit seem to hang suspended on the vertical planes that guarantee the composition's stability by establishing a relationship with the vertical band in the background. The skill with which the artist utilizes the flatness of the support is remarkable.

The asymmetrical shape of the carafe is the result of the need to adjust its left side to the gentle curve created by a fold in the cloth and a piece of fruit that can be seen behind. The glass and carafe are the focal point around which the rest of the composition is constructed. A concentration of light causes a break in the ellipsis of the glass's rim, without destroying its volume. In his desire to transcribe faithfully what he perceived, Cézanne was obliged to introduce deformations that indicate the true nature of painting: the abstract reconstruction of a combination of sensations initiated by the physical world.

Still Life with Putto, c.1895

71 × 57cm, Courtauld Institute, London

To judge by the titles of his works, Cézanne never – unlike numerous other painters – created an image representing 'the artist's studio'. However, a careful examination of the work reproduced here, which is usually classified as a still life, reveals it to be apparently just such a view. Predominant among the various rather odd elements it brings together are several works of art.

A plaster cast of a *Cupid* by Puget, which is in the Louvre, fills the centre of the composition. The presence of this piece, which Cézanne sketched many times, is an expression of the artist's taste for baroque forms and his habit of studying poses from sculpture rather than from live models. This practice is also alluded to by the painting seen leaning against the wall in the background: it is a painted copy of a cast of *Anatomy*, attributed to Michelangelo. These two casts, which are still in Cézanne's studio at Les Lauvres, provide initial indirect references to the work of the absent artist.

On the table, at the feet of the Cupid, he has depicted the 'remains' of a still life – apples and onions (see p. 107) – and, in the lower left-hand corner, the blue carpet that appears in many of his works, including the one featuring the peppermint bottle (see p. 101). This same carpet is also represented in the painting shown propped against the wall to the left. Through a subtle compositional strategy, Cézanne has succeeded, in this 'painting within a painting', in blurring the distinction between the two juxtaposed occurrences, of the carpet. This device, coupled with the positioning towards the rear of a green apple the same size as those in the immediate foreground, has the effect of leaving the viewer with a feeling of some ambiguity.

Meyer Schapiro has laid a great deal of emphasis on the latent eroticism of this image (Schapiro, 1978, pp. 1–4). But all the studio objects depicted have been integrated into a highly complex spatial construction of inclined planes that combines several different visual readings (from front to back, from bottom to top, and a high-angle view from top to bottom) and that achieves equilibrium in spite of taking little account of the laws of statics. This integration seems to indicate, rather, that Cézanne is presenting us simultaneously with an image of his studio as a workplace and his vision of still life as the ideal medium in which to meditate on the transformation of nature into painting.

The Lake at Annecy, 1896

64 × 81.3cm, Courtauld Institute, London

In 1896, following a month-long cure at Vichy, Cézanne underwent a period of enforced rest at the Hôtel de l'Abbaye in Talloires, on the banks of Lake Annecy. While there, he wrote to Joachim Gasquet, a poet from Aix whom he had met the previous April: 'Here I am far away from our dear Provence for a while. After some hesitation, my family – in whose hands I now find myself – has decided to settle me temporarily in this spot. It is a temperate zone. The altitude of the surrounding hills is quite pronounced. The lake, at this place confined between two gullies, seems suited to the drawing exercises of young ladies. It's still nature, of course, but a bit like what we are used to seeing in the travel journals of young girls.' (Letter dated 21 July 1896.)

Three days later, his homesickness was becoming unbearable. He wrote to his friend Solari: 'When I was in Aix, it seemed to me I would be better elsewhere. But now I am here, I long for Aix. Life is starting to be of the most deadly monotony . . . to distract myself I paint, which is not much fun, but the lake is very nice with big hills all around, as high as two thousand metres they tell me; it's not as fine as our countryside, but it's not bad.' (Letter dated 23 July 1896.) This view of the Château de Duingt seen from Talloires is the only painting resulting from this trip. Once back in Provence, Cézanne rarely left it again.

While the rather dark colour harmonies seen here are similar to those the artist employed in his northern works, the rendering of the subject itself, with its closed space and opaque, highly-constructed reflections in the water, relates it more closely to the *Bridge at Maincy* (p.69).

Still Life with Onions, c.1896–8

66 × 82cm, Musée d'Orsay, Paris

Unlike some of the other still lifes, in which the arbitrary nature of the subject emphasizes its submission to the laws of painting, this one is notable for its simplicity and a feeling of naturalism in the grouping of the objects, all of which might easily appear on a kitchen table during the preparation of a meal. But what Cézanne is offering us is, once again, an insight into the world of painting.

The device of the knife, placed at an angle to create a slight impression of depth, is a 'quotation' from Manet, who himself borrowed it from Chardin. The artificially raised plate permits the artist to show the volumes from high up, thus accentuating their roundness. The onions provided a pretext for the introduction of a pink shade modulated with yellow, a colour which recurs throughout the painting, sometimes on the surface, sometimes with a certain depth. A break in the rim of the glass underlines the object's 'drawn' character.

The pronounced animation of the paint layer forming the ground, in the greenish blue tone so dear to Cézanne, is attained through a discontinuous brushstroke; the remarkable effects of transparency in this area are the result of his – by then – considerable experience with water-colour.

Road to Mas Jolie at the Château-Noir, c.1895–1900

79.5 × 64.5cm, Galerie Beyeler, Basel

One need only compare this canvas with *Winding Road in Provence* (p. 51) to understand just how far Cézanne travelled in thirty years and just how radically his work differs from that of the Impressionists. This painting does not represent the instantaneous perception of a woodland track, but a painstaking reconstruction, based on a multitude of sensations analysed exhaustively to arrive at precisely the right tones. The aim is not to repeat nature, but to make us see it as if for the very first time. And to achieve his aim, Cézanne cannot rely solely on his vision: he must convey his sensations.

The barely sketched shapes of the trees are spread out delicately across a surface iridescent with glowing colours, which are built up in individual dabs (one per colour) to convey the right sensation. The broad, almost square stroke developed in the water-colours is combined here in a quite new way with the hatched stroke that evolved during the early 1880s (see p. 77).

The converging lines of the road are blurred by patches of colour. More clear is the series of horizontals which, while remaining parallel to the picture plane, become progressively shorter until they finally disappear. With this device Cézanne creates a simultaneous effect of depth and frontality, which is the source of the marked feeling of movement conveyed by the work.

Mont Sainte-Victoire, c.1897

45 × 46cm, Institute of Arts, Detroit

The spreading areas of colour representing the pine branches that frame this view seem to draw apart like curtains to reveal Sainte-Victoire, reposing majestically and immutably on its geological foundations. Patches of light ochre curve up from the bottom of the canvas, passing over two fine ridges to reach the summit. The work's almost *tachiste* construction has the effect of making the mountain appear dramatically before us, the instant we look at the painting. Cézanne has imbued the work with a remarkable liveliness by means of a variety of upward-moving strokes, and it is towards the top that the contrasts between warm and cold colours are at their most subtle.

A series of fine blue strokes directs the eye and, almost as if we are ourselves parting the branches, prepares it for the breathtakingly close-up vision of the mountain.

The peak's silhouette is the same as the one that appears in *The Château-Noir and Mont Sainte-Victoire* (p. 117) indicating that the work was painted from somewhere near the Château-Noir.

Self-portrait with Beret, c.1898–1900

64 × 53.5cm, Museum of Fine Arts, Boston

This is Cézanne's final self-portrait, painted when he was approaching his sixties, white-haired but still robust. The portrait is very like some of the last photographs we have of the artist, taken by Émile Bernard during his visit to the Les Lauves studio in 1904–5. Rewald has pointed out that the red chair seen here also appears in the portrait of Madame Cézanne (p. 67) dating from about 1877 (Rewald, 1978 [exhib. cat.], p. 73). This self-portrait may have been executed in the apartment on the rue Hégésippe-Moreau, in Paris, which the artist rented in 1899 after having been obliged to sell the Jas de Bouffan following the death of his mother. It was here, in any case, that later in the year he painted his portrait of Ambroise Vollard (p. 119).

A brief sketch, visible beneath the thin pigment layer, serves to position the various elements the artist saw reflected in his mirror. Remaining firmly within the limits of the drawing, the remarkable economical compositon consists fundamentally of the three arcs created by the beret, the shoulders and left arm, and the back of the chair.

The thinness of the paint layer across the whole surface helps to throw into relief the artist's face, which is the only part of the painting to have been worked in any detail. In his exercises in self-confrontation, Cézanne always depicted himself with great assurance (see p. 73). Here he seems distant, perhaps, but serene and confident; for his eternally nagging doubt, 'Will I achieve my longed-for goal?' actually served as a kind of catalyst. The poet Rainer Maria Rilke understood what lay behind the artist's attitude of detachment: ' . . . it is the labour at which Cézanne's furious male will burned itself out over thirty-five years of his life; to advance even for a few paces on the path of his passion, he was obliged to turn aside from everything, not with disdain, but with the heroism of someone who chooses the appearance of death through love of life' (Rainer Maria Rilke, *Lettres françaises à Merline* [Paris: Seuil, 1950], p. 81; letter dated 20 February 1921).

The Millstone in the Park of the Château-Noir, c.1898–1900

73 × 92cm, Museum of Fine Art, Philadelphia

During the 1890s, Cézanne had noticed on the road to Le Tholonet a strange building with narrow Gothic windows (see p. 117), marvellously situated, surrounded by forest and constructed in the yellow stone produced at the Bibémus quarry. As Rewald has pointed out, the property's name of 'Château-Noir' (Black Castle) is a misnomer that stems from the legend that its first owner was a coal merchant who had it painted black (Rewald, 1978 [exhib. cat.], p. 27]. Another tale asserts that he was an alchemist, which accounts for the even more forbidding nickname of 'Château du Diable' (Devil's Castle).

Cézanne must certainly have wandered through the woods surrounding the Château-Noir as, in the past, he had through the forest of Fontainebleau, searching for 'subjects to explore'. Deep among the trees, the filtered light offered him the ever-fresh pleasure of striving to get the tone exactly right, of finding just the desired 'passage' to link two values.

Rewald actually discovered the motif depicted here, unchanged, in 1935, and a photo he took at the time provides evidence of the extreme fidelity with which Cézanne rendered the scene (Rewald, 1978 [exhib. cat.], p. 27); the millstone and the other blocks appear in the painting exactly as they did in reality. This same literalness of representation is also found in many studies of forest interiors and of the rocks at the Bibémus quarry. Preparing, as he was, to embark on the ambitious compositions of *The Large Bathers*, the artist no doubt felt the need of the sustenance provided by direct contact with nature.

The Château-Noir and Mont Sainte-Victoire, c.1904–6

66.1 × 82cm, Bridgestone Museum, Tokyo

There are many striking views to be seen of the Château-Noir (p. 129) and Mont Sainte-Victoire (p. 111) as one wanders through the surrounding forest. This, however, is the only painting that combines in a broad panorama the two subjects that preoccupied Cézanne most intensely during his final years. He tried out several viewpoints before arriving at the form that allowed him to render his sensation of the combined subject most effectively. As he confided to his friend Louis Aurenche, he had nothing but his painting through which to pursue and eventually discover the form that conveyed the intensity of his sensation: 'You speak in your letter of my accomplishment in art. I believe I am achieving a little more each day, although somewhat painfully. For while a strong sensation of nature – and this I have most acutely – is the necessary basis of all conception of art, and the foundation of the grandeur and beauty of any future work, knowledge of the means of expressing one's emotion is no less essential, and can only be acquired after a great deal of experience.' (Cézanne, *Correspondance*, p. 198.)

These words were written around the time this painting was done. Cézanne makes clear reference to his <u>sensation</u> – rather than his vision – of nature. Sensation is a primal form of 'presence-in-the-world', involving the whole body and not simply vision. (The philosophical investigations of Maurice Merleau-Ponty contained in *Le Visible et l'invisible* [Paris: Gallimard, 1964] and, particularly, the more recent work of Henry Maldiney entitled *Art et Existence* [Paris: Klincksieck, 1985] offer analyses that are basic to a phenomenological understanding of Cézanne's painting.) Basically, Cézanne apprehends the world through colour, through what he calls 'colour sensations'. Each stroke applied to the canvas must be a direct extension of his sensations. It is for this reason that his painting is a painting of presence-in-the-world and not of representation of the world. The painter's presence-in-the-world via his colour sensations is, moreover, the only explanation for the overall tonal similarity between two works so chronologically and iconographically distant as this painting and *Boat and Bathers* (p. 99). In both cases, the artist does not paint the light: the light emanates from the painting.

Portrait of Ambroise Vollard, 1899

100 × 81cm, Musée du Petit Palais, Paris

While not entirely finished, this portrait of Vollard is nevertheless nearer completion than the one of Geffroy (Musée d'Orsay, Paris), which Cézanne felt obliged to abandon in 1895, discouraged – in spite of the considerable number of sittings already imposed on the critic – by his lack of progress. For reasons that still remain obscure, the same fate was meted out to the portrait of Cézanne's Aix friend, Joachim Gasquet (National Gallery, Prague).

This portrait was undertaken at the famous dealer's own request. While the anecdotal aspects of Vollard's reminiscences (1914) must generally be approached with some circumspection, certain extracts serve to throw light on the painter's work methods and on the legendary lack of mercy he showed his models.

. . . One day I ventured to ask him to paint my portrait. He consented at once, and arranged a sitting at his studio in rue Hégésippe-Moreau for the following day. Upon arriving, I saw a chair in the middle of the studio, arranged on a packing case, which was in turn supported by four rickety legs. I surveyed this platform with misgiving. Cézanne divined my apprehension. 'I prepared the model stand with my own hands. Oh, you won't run the least risk of falling, Monsieur Vollard, if you just keep your balance. Anyway, you mustn't budge an inch when you pose!' Seated at last – and with what pains! – I took great care not to make a single false move; in fact I sat absolutely motionless; but my very immobility eventually brought on a drowsiness against which I successfully struggled for some time. At last, however, my head dropped over onto my shoulder, the balance was destroyed, and the chair, the packing and I all crashed to the floor together! Cézanne rushed over to me. 'You wretch! You've spoiled the pose. Do I have to tell you again you must sit like an apple? Does an apple move?'

Further on, Vollard writes:

The solidity of Cézanne's painting is readily explained when one knows his method of working. Because he did not paint with a thick impasto, but put one layer of paint as thin as water-colour over another, the paint dried instantly; he never had to fear that movement within the paint itself, which gives rise to cracks when the upper and lower layers dry at different rates. (Ambroise Vollard, Cézanne [Paris, Crès, 1919, pp. 123–4 and 131–2.)

Still Life, c.1900

55 × 46cm, National Gallery of Art, Washington

Of all Cézanne's 'confidences' recorded by Émile Bernard during his visits to Aix and collected in his 'Souvenirs sur Paul Cézanne', published in *Mercure de France* after the artist's death, there is one that is worth quoting in relation to this painting: 'Drawing and colour are not separate; while one paints, one draws; the more the colour harmonizes, the more precise becomes the drawing. When the colour is rich, the form is at its height. The contrasts and relations of tone hold the secret of drawing and form.' (Doran, 1978, p. 63.) The point, as Cézanne remarked to Maurice Denis, was to 'create form with the paintbrush'.

Here, owing to the extreme simplicity of the composition, the viewer's full attention is absorbed by the work's extraordinary chromatic richness. Most striking of all is the precision with which the blue strokes are applied, accentuating volumes without enclosing them and ensuring the liaison between different values.

Surely no other painter has possessed such a finely tuned sense of reality. And it is to this acuity that we always return in attempting to understand Cézanne's painting. As he explained in his first letter to Bernard: '. . . Nature, for us humans, is more in depth than on the surface, which is why we must introduce into our vibrations of light, represented by reds and yellows, a sufficient number of bluish hues to convey a feeling of the air' (Cézanne, *Correspondance*, p. 300). Unlike the Impressionists, Cézanne was not attempting to render objectively the effects of light on his retina, for he knew full well that this would dissipate the volumes he wished so fiercely to preserve.

Bathers, c.1899–1904

51.3 × 61.7cm, The Art Institute of Chicago, Illinois

The long series of studies of bathers, male and female, on which Cézanne had been working since the 1870s eventually culminated in a few small paintings dating from after 1890. The harmony between the nude figure and a landscape setting after which he was clearly striving in these works is visibly more successfully achieved when he abandons a geometric construction of space in favour of a more 'baroque', more open space, much closer to the one he admired in the work of Delacroix.

Here, the whole surface of the canvas is animated by an impalpable tremor, conveyed both by the subtle vibrating of the bodies – achieved through the repeated but invariably incomplete outlines – and the isolated touches of green, prussian blue, colbalt and ultramarine that cover the surface, obliterating contours and unifying the space.

Portrait of a Peasant, c.1900

92.7 × 73.7cm, National Gallery of Canada, Ottawa

For his famous series of works depicting groups of card players, painted in the early 1890s, Cézanne took as models the peasants and labourers who worked on the family property of the Jas de Bouffan. The artist declared to Vollard that 'The goal of all art is the human face', and he was to return to these familiar characters many times in the numerous portraits created during the last decade of his career.

Cézanne's letters occasionally include references to particular difficulties he was experiencing: 'The reading of the model and its realization are sometimes slow in coming', he wrote to Camoin in 1904. His goal was not to render fleeting facial expressions, but rather to reveal through exhaustive analysis the unique and permanent nature of each of his models. The portraits from this period all share the same marked stability and monumentality. Here, the extremely mobile ground, enlivened by discontinuous strokes of blue and green, accentuates the extraordinary physical presence of the model.

Mont Sainte-Victoire, c.1903–4

83.8 × 65cm, Art Museum, Princeton

In 1902, Cézanne moved into the new studio he had had built at Les Lauves, just north of Aix-en-Provence, and began work on *Large Bathers*. He did not actually live there, but went each day to paint. When the weather was fine, he had simply to make the short climb to the crest of Les Lauves to see, spread before him, the most splendid view of Mont Sainte-Victoire.

From this spot, as Rewald has pointed out, the mountain's imposing profile 'appears like an irregular triangle whose long side rises gently up to the sharp peak, which then descends precipitously towards the flat top of Mont du Cengle. At Cézanne's feet was the vast and rolling plain with its grid of fields . . . ' (Rewald, 1978 [exhib. cat.], p. 33.) The eight pictures Cézanne painted from this promontory constitute the climax of his intensive investigations, started in 1885, aimed at understanding and liberating all the energy contained in this landscape.

The view looking down upon the plain, whose depth is accentuated by the strong foreground element, is held for only an instant. For this frontal element possesses a double and somewhat paradoxical function: to create depth and then to bring the second plane back towards the first. This effect is created by the element's ochre colour, which by echoing the ochre areas of the plain prevents them from receding into the distance. The main subject is presented to us with the verticality of a wall, but the viewer's gaze is forced to operate simultaneously in perspective and on the surface.

The highly articulated and extremely mobile space thus created 'supports' a mountain that seems to burst forth from the horizontal plain, the open outline of its double profile thrusting it perpetually skyward.

The Château-Noir, c.1904

74 × 94cm, Musée Picasso, Paris

Cézanne still continued to work at the Château-Noir after his move to the Les Lauves studio. This painting is a view from the west, showing the building and the terrace. There are four versions of the Château seen from this angle, one of which belonged to Monet. Like all of them, the one seen here – which was owned by Picasso – does not show Mont Sainte-Victoire, which remains hidden by the building.

If we look back at the work entitled *Road at Auvers-sur-Oise* (p. 59) we can see to what extent it was Cézanne's relentless determination to 'explore the subject' that led him to develop his unique style. Here, the brushstrokes seem to form a web of colour. The modulated blues, greens and violets applied diagonally in the sky are attentuated reflections of the foreground colours; this lends a harmony to the composition very like the harmony of sounds attained in the art of the fugue.

This canvas, which seems at first glance to operate entirely on the surface, is actually activated in depth by colours that can be glimpsed through the whole of the upper pigment layer. Structured with assurance and determination, this layer nevertheless trembles, pulsates, vibrates. Cézanne's great emotion before 'the pure appearance' of nature, although carefully contained, permeates this painting utterly.

The Large Bathers, c.1902–6

130 × 193cm, National Gallery, London

According to reports from those close to him, Cézanne began in 1895 to paint pictures much larger than anything he had produced since his Salon submissions of 1870. He had never given up his idea of one day doing a 'large museum painting', and this is perhaps why the bathers theme was among his most regular subjects. It may also be for this reason that he chose to draw upon his repertoire of 'classical' poses, carefully recorded in his sketchbooks since his youth during study sessions at the Louvre. Research by Reff and Krumrine has enabled us to identify many of the sculptures from which these poses are derived.

While Émile Bernard attributed Cézanne's forgoing of studies from live models to a hypothetical 'fear of women' or to religious scruples, it seems more likely that suitable models were simply not available in Aix. Moreover, the artist undoubtedly felt much much at ease working with poses that he had perfected over many years. For he was very conscious of his own limitations and often admitted in his letters that drawing from life presented him with enormous problems.

When the nude is represented simply as a flux of colour, floating among the indefinite greens and blues of a landscape (see pp. 99 and 123) – which is especially the case in the water-colours – formal integration can be achieved through a rhythmic ordering. In large-scale paintings, however, the artist is obliged to modify the body's proportions in order to integrate it successfully into the composition. In this work, the figures' dimensions have been considerably altered: the arms, the torsos, the legs, have nearly all been elongated or shortened, resulting in deformations that are otherwise difficult to explain.

Difficult to explain, also, is the introduction of a dog and a few apples towards the centre of the composition, which seems to indicate a return to the 'narrativity' of early works (*Le Déjeuner sur l'herbe* and *Pastoral*). Krumrine has justly drawn attention to the presence, on the extreme right, of a mysterious, apparently meditative figure, who seems to have been added as an afterthought. A convincing interpretation of this character has yet to be formulated.

View of Mont Sainte-Victoire from Les Lauves, c.1902–6

63.5 × 83cm, Kunsthaus, Zurich

'I owe you the truth about painting', Cézanne wrote to Émile Bernard, 'And I shall tell it to you.' A year later, in September 1906, only shortly before his death, Cézanne confided to his son his disappointment with his 'hapless' correspondent, who had bombarded him with questions without, apparently, having learnt very much: ' . . . we agree on this point, he's an intellectual, chock-full of museum recollections, but he doesn't see enough in nature, and it's the main point – to get out of school, all schools' (Cézanne, *Correspondance*, p. 328).

The ageing artist realized, in spite of everything, that he had created a new type of painting; he had succeeded in changing the rules and even in eliminating them altogether to make way for his eternally repeated affirmation of the 'sensations that we carry with us at birth', unique to each of us, which in painting can only be realized through a genuine contact with nature.

Here, then, Mont Sainte-Victoire propels itself upward through the diversely modulated colours and 'passages' that provide the building-blocks for the composition's overall unity. The areas left uncovered imbue the mountain with an extraordinary lightness. The whole landscape seems to be expanding. Indeed, one need only examine a photograph to see that the mountain stretches across an expressive space in the painting far wider than the one it fills in reality.

View of Mont Sainte-Victoire from Les Lauves, c.1904–6

60 × 72cm, Kunstmuseum, Basel

This canvas represents the zenith of Cézanne's *oeuvre*, in some sense a synthesis and a completion of all his other works. Never has the act of painting reached such heights. And never has any analysis attained the discernment of Henri Maldiney's definitive text. (Henri Maldiney, 'Cézanne et Sainte-Victoire. Peinture et vérité', *Sainte-Victoire. Cézanne. 1990* [Aix-en-Provence, Musée Granet]).

'One sees a painting the first time or one never sees it at all,' said Cézanne. First, this Mont Sainte-Victoire begins blue. And with the blue, the space. The space begins blue in a diagonal track from the bottom of the painting to the sky, travelling through the pale blues, gentle but radiant, of the plain. These link delicately with those of the mountain and are drawn to the great spread blues that bathe the crest and echo as blue patches, suspended in the sky. The gaze is splintered into a multiplicity of paths whose various forces interact in a to-and-fro of opposing tensions.

This interaction awakens the bright greens of the plain, revealed as the light-bearing colour, more on the earth than in the sky . . . were it not that the sky lies, in the green, stretched upon the earth. These greens rise up in successive broken tiers, which broaden on the right up to the horizon, where they modulate with the greens of the sky – carried aloft by the mountain.

While the chromatic density of the painting is extraordinary, it is the whites that play the most delicate role:

The gaps that pierce the dim, dark waves of green towards the sides are reverberations of the great central lightness, whose power depends upon these flashes. All these median whites are attuned to the sovereign white of the summit, which reflects in all the whites of the mountain. And where the contacts are slender and fragile between the blues, the red ochres and the greens, these fine whites, sometimes mere points, always intense, prevent fusion and continuity.

The Large Bathers, c.1906

208 × 249cm, Museum of Art, Philadelphia

While this picture was the last (and the largest) of the three works on this theme painted by Cézanne after 1895, it was left unfinished at his death, and it is hard to see it as the culmination point of his *oeuvre* as a whole. It forces us to recognize that the problem of the integration of the nude figure into a landscape setting, with which he grappled all his life, is even harder to resolve in a large work, as comparison of this painting with *Boat and Bathers* (p. 99) and *Bathers* (p. 123) illustrates. On the other hand, the extremely austere composition demonstrates a greater clarity and stability than the London canvas (p. 131) and, being unfinished, is much lighter.

Cézanne's paintings of bathers have inspired an extraordinary number of studies, ranging from strictly formal analyses to conjectures of quite breathtaking implausibility. The latter purport to discern in the works all sorts of hidden images, usually indecent, that give rise to a plethora of vaguely psychoanalytical speculation, frequently combined with an extremely elaborate network of references to classical Renaissance iconography.

The true motives that drove Cézanne to return to this theme again and again throughout his life will never be known, for they were never revealed. But the artist did not hide his admiration for traditional art, nor his desire to be accepted one day into 'Bouguereau's Salon'. His continuing preoccupation with the Salon was linked to his wish to be finally recognized by his fellow-inhabitants of Aix, who had always held him in contempt. On the question of how important it was for Cézanne to situate himself within the great tradition of Western art, a letter he wrote in January 1905 to Roger Marx, editor of the extremely influential *Gazette des Beaux-arts*, is instructive:

> My age and my health will never allow me to realize the dream of art that I have been pursuing all my life . . . To my mind one does not substitute oneself for the past, one merely adds a new link to its chain. With the temperament of a painter and an ideal of art – that is to say conception of nature – sufficient means of expression would have been necessary to be intelligible to the general public and to occupy a decent position in the history of art. (Cézanne, *Correspondance*, pp. 311–12.)

Cézanne's innovations, particularly in the water-colours, did not all have the repercussions that might have been expected. Moreover, the direct links that have been established in art history between certain of his works and the origins of Cubism require re-examination. Cézanne's painting as a link in the historical chain leads rather, on reflection, towards Matisse (via the nudes) and Klee (via his techniques of modulation.)

Still Life with Pomegranates, Carafe, Sugar Bowl, Bottle and Water Melon, c.1900–06

30 × 40cm, Musée du Louvre, cabinet des dessins, Paris

Cézanne, who had been making watercolours for a number of years, appears to have attached increasing importance to the medium from 1895 on – at least if we are to judge by the quantity he produced. As Götz Adriani has noted: 'We may certainly see the influence of Ambroise Vollard as another cause of the amazing burgeoning of his final decade. For it is very possible that, for commercial reasons, the energetic Paris art dealer encouraged the painter to produce watercolours – which were quicker to execute – and to pay more attention than before to the results obtained. Vollard recalled only too well discovering, on his first visit to Aix in 1806, a large cardboard box full of watercolours left lying casually on the floor.' (Adriani, 1981, p. 59)

Whatever the reason for this proliferation, the real interest of these final works lies in their exemplary character; for each one represents a 'culmination point' of what Cézanne was striving to achieve all his life. All the themes he had explored over the previous thirty years were treated again in the watercolours, and with a mastery hitherto unequalled – a fact that can be grasped through a comparison of this work with *Still Life with Chest* (p. 81), which features the same sugar bowl among its compositional elements.

The transparency of the medium and the radiance resulting from the white paper left uncovered enabled the artist to obtain an expansion of the volumes and a spatiality that are quite without precedent. The transparency of the watercolours itself allows us to perceive his method of chromatic modulation. This term 'modulation', of which Cézanne was so fond, is used in music to describe the transition from one tonality to another. Here, the curves of the bottle, the sugar bowl and the melon are rendered by the juxtaposition of areas of varying tonalities – blue, sea green and purple – with indefinite contours; and the same technique is employed for the pomegranates, only using yellow and red. The symbiosis between line and colour is such that they are no longer distinguishable: the motif is created in its entirety by the rhythmic unfurling of the colour, which draws and modulates simultaneously.

CHRONOLOGY

1839

Birth on 19 January in Aix-en-Provence, of Paul Cézanne, eldest son of Louis-Auguste Cézanne, hat maker, and of Anne-Elisabeth-Honorine Aubert. He starts primary school in 1844.

1848

His father takes over the bankrupt Banque Barges and, with an associate, establishes Aix's only bank, the Banque Cézanne et Cabassol, thus securing his financial position.

1852–1858

Cézanne enters the Collège Bourbon in Aix, where he becomes friendly with Émile Zola and Batistin Baille, whose literary and artistic tastes he shares.

1857

While completing his studies, Cézanne registers at the Free Municipal School for Drawing, in Aix, where he meets Philippe Solari, Numa Coste and Achille Emperaire.

1858

Begins corresponding with Zola, who has been in Paris since February. In November Cézanne passes the baccalaureat. Continues taking drawing classes at the Free Municipal School until 1862.

1859

Under pressure from his father, enrols in the law school of the University of Aix. Louis-Auguste Cézanne acquires an eighteenth-century residence, Jas de Bouffan, in the countryside outside Aix. Zola encourages him in his desire to become a painter and presses Cézanne to join him in Paris.

1861

Cézanne abandons his law studies and finally spends a few months in Paris (April to September). With Zola, he visits the Salon, the Louvre and the Luxembourg. Registers at the Académie Suisse, where he meets Pissarro. Discouraged by his lack of progress, returns to Aix and begins working in his father's bank; takes evening classes at The Free Municipal School of Drawing.

1862

Leaves the bank once and for all and takes up painting again. Zola and Baille spend their summer holidays with him. Returns in the autumn to Paris, where he fails the entrance examination for the École des Beaux-Arts.

1863

Cézanne works at the Académie Suisse, where he meets Guillemet and Guillaumin. Exhibits at the Salon des Refusés.

1864

Works at copying Old Masters in the Louvre and at the Luxembourg. Until the war of 1870, spends winters in Paris and summers in Aix, where he becomes friendly with Valabrégue (1865) and Alexis (1868). Executes dark-tone paintings with erotic overtones. In spite of annual attempts, his paintings continue to be refused by the Salon. In Paris, meets artists' model Hortense Fiquet (1869).

1870

At the outbreak of the Franco-Prussian War, Cézanne returns to Aix to avoid the draft. Reluctant to admit his liaison with Hortense Fiquet to his father, who is still providing him with a monthly allowance, he spends the major part of the war with her in L'Estaque.

1872

Birth of his son Paul in Paris, where he has been since the autumn of 1871. In the spring, settles with his family at the Hôtel du Grand Cerf, near Pontoise, so as to be able to work with Pissarro. Sees Guillaumin frequently. Moves in the autumn to Auvers-sur-Oise, where he remains until 1874 and where he meets Dr Gachet.

1873

Père Tanguy opens his famous shop in Paris, where he exhibits the work of young painters. Cézanne is among them. Art critic Théodore Duret shows an interest in his work.

1874

Encouraged by Pissarro, presents works at the first Impressionist exhibition, held at Nadar's studio. Count Doria purchases one of his canvases – *The House of the Hanged Man*. By the autumn, Cézanne is back in Paris; works with Guillaumin, now his neighbour.

1875

Through Renoir, meets Victor Chocquet, who becomes an ardent defender of his work.

1876

Cézanne spends most of the year in L'Estaque; does not take part in the second Impressionist exhibition. Back in Paris in the autumn, works once again with Guillaumin.

1877

Participates in the third Impressionist exhibition, presenting sixteen paintings. With the exception of Georges Rivière, the critics are very harsh. In search of subjects, Cézanne travels throughout the area surrounding Paris: Pointoise, Auvers, Chantilly, Fontainebleau.

1878
Installs Hortense Fiquet in Marseilles, near Monticelli's home, and spends the year travelling between Aix and L'Estaque. Financial difficulties result from the quarrel with his father; Zola helps him out.

1879
Back in Paris once again in the spring, Cézanne settles this time in Melun, whence he visits Zola, who had the previous year purchased a house in Médan, near St Germain-en-Laye. Cézanne returns to Paris in the spring of 1880, making annual visits to Médan until 1882.

1882
Works early in the year with Renoir in L'Estaque, then returns to Paris. One of his works is finally accepted by the Salon. In October, returns to Aix and settles down at the Jas de Bouffan, which he leaves only to make occasional visits to friends. Works in the countryside around Aix, painting and drawing; continues to submit works to the Salon, without success.

1886
In March, Zola publishes *L'Oeuvre*, a novel describing the life and suicide of an unsuccessful painter. Deeply hurt by the character of Claude Lantier, Cézanne breaks off a long-standing friendship with the author. With the consent of his father, who dies shortly afterwards, the artist marries Hortense Fique in April. His financial worries are at an end.

1889
Starting the previous year, spends several months in Paris. He is invited to exhibit in the Salon des XX, in Brussels. His works are mentioned in *Le Moderniste illustré*, published by Aurier.

1890
Makes a five-month trip to Switzerland with his family. Back in Aix, Cézanne suffers the early symptoms of diabetes.

1892
Continues to divide his time between Aix and Paris, and works occasionally in the Forêt de Fontainebleau.

1894
His paintings fetch reasonable prices at the auctions of Duret's and Père Tanguy's collections. Several are purchased by the young Ambroise Vollard, who has recently opened a gallery on the Rue Laffitte. At Monet's birthday celebration, at Giverny, Cézanne meets Clémenceau, Geffroy and Rodin.

1895
Having spent the first half of the year in Paris, returns to Aix; rents a small hut in the Bibemus quarry, to which he makes many excursions. In November, holds his first one-man exhibition at Vollard's gallery (150 paintings). Two of his works enter the Musée du Luxembourg as part of the Caillebotte bequest.

1896
Cézanne is introduced to Edmond Jaloux and Louis Aurenche by the young poet Joachim Gasquet. Following medical treatment at Vichy, he spends the summer at Talloires, on the shores of Lake Annecy, before returning to Paris.

1897
Having spent the months from January to April in Paris, works again in the Forêt de Fontainebleau, and then in Aix and Le Tholonet. His mother dies in the autumn.

1898
Cézanne works at the Château-Noir, halfway between Aix and Le Tholonet; returns later to Paris, where he spends most of the following year, working sometimes in Pontoise and sometimes in the Forêt de Fontainebleau.

1899
Returns to Aix in the autumn; is obliged to sell the Jas de Bouffan in order to divide the inheritance. Durand-Ruel buys a number of works by Cézanne at the Chocquet sale. In December, Vollard gives him another one-man show and purchases the entire contents of his studio.

1900
Cézanne rents an apartment in Aix and remains in the town most of the year. Through the influence of Roger Marx, three of his paintings are exhibited in the Centennale de l'Art français held on the occasion of the Exposition Universelle. Durand-Ruel arranges for him to show works at the Cassirer gallery, in Berlin.

1901
Buys a hillside plot on the road to Les Lauves, with a view of Aix and Sainte-Victoire, on which he builds a studio. Exhibits at the Salon des Indépendants in Paris and at the Salon de la Libre Esthétique in Brussels. Meets Léo Larguier and Charles Camoin, who are completing their military services in Aix.

1902
Very touched by the death of Zola, in spite of their estrangement; spends some time in the Cevennes at Larguier's home. Moves into his new studio.

1904
Is visited by Émile Bernard and subsequently corresponds with him.

Cézanne makes his last trip to Paris and goes once again to work in Fontainebleau. Exhibits works at the Salon d'Automne and again at Cassirer's gallery in Berlin; also at the Salon de la Libre Esthétique in Brussels.

1905
Exhibits water-colours at Vollard's gallery in the spring, and shows again at the Salon d'Automne.

1906
Cézanne's health deteriorates throughout the year. Caught in a sudden storm on 15 October while working outdoors, he returns home soaked; dies on 23 October in his apartment on the Rue Boulegon.

SELECT BIBLIOGRAPHY

Writings by Cézanne
Paul Cézanne: Correspondance, collected, annotated and with a preface by John Rewald. Paris: Grasset, 1937; new, updated and expanded edition, 1978.

Works on Cézanne
ADRIANI, Götz. *Cézanne: Aquarelles*, translated from the German. Freiburg: Office du Livre, 1981.

BADT, Kurt. *Die Kunst Cézannes*. Munich: Prestel-Verlag, 1956.

BRION-GUERRY, Liliane. *Cézanne et l'expression de l'espace*. Paris: Flammarion, 1950; new, updated and corrected edition, Paris: Albin Michel, 1966.

CHAPPUIS, Adrien. *The Drawings of Paul Cézanne. A Catalogue raisonné*. 2 vols. London: Thames and Hudson, and Greenwich, Conn.: New York Graphic Society, 1973.

DORAN, P. Michael. *Conversations avec Cézanne, Émile Bernard, Jules Borély, Maurice Denis, Joachim Gasquet, Gustave Geffroy, Francis Jourdain, Léo Larguier, Karl Ernst Osthaus, R.P. Rivière et J.F. Schnerb, Ambroise Vollard*, commentary translated from the English. Paris: Macula, 1978.

FRY, Roger. *Cézanne. A Study of his Development*. London: Hogarth, and New York: Macmillan, 1927; new edition, 1952.

MONNERET, Sophie. *Cézanne, Zola . . . La fraternité du génie*. Paris: Denoël, 1978.

NOVOTNY, Fritz. *Cézanne und das Ende der wissenschaftlichen Perspektive*. Vienna: Anton Schroll & Co., 1938.

REFF, Theodore. 'Cézanne et Poussin'. *Journal of the Warburg and Courtauld Institute*, vol. XVIII, January 1960, pp. 150–74

—— 'Cézanne, Flaubert, St Anthony, and the Queen of Sheba'. *The Art Bulletin*, vol. XLIV, 1962, pp. 113–25.

—— 'The Pictures within Cézanne's Pictures'. *Arts Magazine*, June 1979, pp. 90–104.

—— 'Cézanne's "Cardplayers" and their Sources'. *Arts Magazine*, vol. 55, no. 5, November 1980, pp. 104–17.

—— 'Cézanne et la perspective: quelques remarques à la lumière de documents nouveaux'. *Revue de l'Art*, no. 86, 1989, pp. 8–15.

REWALD, John. *Les Aquarelles de Cézanne. Catalogue raisonné*, translated from the English. Paris: Arts et Métiers graphiques, 1984.

—— *Cézanne*. Paris: Flammarion, 1986.

SCHAPIRO, Meyer. *Paul Cézanne*. New York: Harry N. Abrams, 1952; new edition, 1973.

—— 'The Apples of Cézanne. An Essay on the Meaning of Still-Life'. *Modern Art, Selected Papers*. New York: Braziller, 1978, pp. 1–45.

SHIFF, Richard. *Cézanne and the End of Impressionism*. Chicago: University of Chicago Press, 1984.

VENTURI, Lionello. *Cézanne, son art, son oeuvre*, translated from the Italian. 2 vols. Paris: Paul Rosenberg, 1936.

—— *Cézanne*, translated from the Italian. Geneva: Skira, 1978.

Principal Exhibition Catalogues
Cézanne, les dernières années (1895–1906), by John Rewald and Adrien Chappuis. Paris: Éditions de la Réunion des Musées nationaux, 1978.

Cézanne: The Late Work, by William Rubin. New York: The Museum of Modern Art. 1977.

Cézanne: The Early Years 1859–1872, by Lawrence Gowing. New York: Harry N. Abrams, 1988.

Paul Cézanne: Les Baigneuses, by Mary Louise Krumrine. Basel: Musée des Beaux-Arts, 10 September–10 December 1989 (published jointly with Albin Michel).

Sainte Victoire, Cézanne, 1990. Aix-en-Provence: Musée Granet et Réunion des Musées nationaux, 16 June–2 September 1990.

LIST OF PLATES

6: *Self-portrait with Palette*, c.1885, oil on canvas, 91.5 × 71.1 cm, Collection of the artist's family, Paris.

7: *Louis-Auguste Cézanne, the Artist's Father, reading "L'Événement"*, 1866, oil on canvas, 200 × 120 cm, National Gallery of Art, Washington.

8: *The Murder*, c.1870, oil on canvas, 65 × 80 cm, Walker Art Gallery, Liverpool.

10: *The Abduction*, 1867, oil on canvas, 90.5 × 117 cm, Keynes Collection, Fitzwilliam Museum, Cambridge.

11: *Portait of Achille Emperaire*, c.1868, oil on canvas, 200 × 122 cm, Musée d'Orsay, Paris.

12: Stock, caricature of Paul Cézanne with the two paintings which were rejected by the Salon jury of 1870, published in an unidentified Paris newspaper.

13: *Young Girl at the Piano*, 1869–71, oil on canvas, 57 × 92 cm, Hermitage Museum, Leningrad.

14: *Portrait of Émile Zola*, 1862, oil on canvas, 26 × 21 cm, Owner and whereabouts unknown.

15: *Portrait of Dr Gachet*, 1873, charcoal, 32 × 21 cm, Cabinet des Dessins, Musée du Louvre, Paris.

16: Photograph of Cézanne and Pissarro in the Auvers region, c.1874.

18: Pissarro, *Portrait of Cézanne*, 1874, oil on canvas, 73 × 59.7 cm, Private Collection, London.

20: Photograph of the House of the Hanged Man at Auvers-sur-Oise

21: *Pissarro Setting out to Paint*, 1872–6, pencil on paper, 21.3 × 12.9 cm, Cabinet des Dessins, Musée du Louvre, Paris.

22: *Entrance of a Farm at Auvers*, c.1873, etching, Bibliothèque Nationale, Paris.

23: *Portrait of Victor Choquet*, 1876–7, oil on canvas, 46 × 36 cm, Private Collection.

25: Photograph of Cézanne setting out to paint in the region of Auvers-sur-Oise, c.1874.

27: *Bend in the Road*, 1879–82, oil on canvas, 59.5 × 72 cm, Museum of Fine Arts, Boston.

28: Photograph of the environs of Aix, with Mont Sainte-Victoire in the background.

29: Sketches and caricatures on a letter from Cézanne to Émile Zola, July 1889, Collection of M. and Mme Leblond-Zola.

30: *Avenue at Jas de Bouffan*, 1884–7, pencil on paper, 30.7 × 47.8 cm, Boynans-van Beuningen Museum, Rotterdam.

31: *Landscape*, 1884–7, pencil on paper, 35 × 54 cm, British Museum, London.

33: *Puget's Cupid*, 1886–9, pencil on paper, 49.2 × 30 cm, Private collection, Cambridge (Mass.).

34: *Hat. Flowers in a carafe*, 1892–6, pencil on paper, 36 × 48 cm, Paul Cassier Collection.

36: *The Boy in the Red Waistcoat*, 1890–5, watercolour, 46.2 × 30.2 cm, Private Collection, Zürich.

37: Photograph of the quarry at Bibémus, c.1950.

38: Photograph of Mont Sainte-Victoire, seen from the terrace at Château-Noir, c.1935.

38: Photograph of The Studio, Les Lauves, c.1904.

39: Photograph of a farm near Gardanne, c.1935.

40: Photograph by Émile Bernard of Cézanne on the hill at Les Lauves, 1904.

45: *Head of an Old Man*, c.1865, oil on canvas, 51 × 48 cm, Musée d'Orsay, Paris.

47: *Still Life with Sugar Pot, Pears and Blue Cup*, c.1866, oil on canvas, 30 × 41 cm, Musée d'Orsay, Paris.

49: *The Negro Scipion*, c.1867, oil on canvas, 107 × 83 cm, Museo de Arte, São Paulo.

51: *Winding Road in Provence*, c.1868, oil on canvas, 91 × 71 cm, The Montreal Museum of Fine Arts.

53: *Paul Alexis Reading to Émile Zola*, c.1869–70, oil on canvas, 130 × 160 cm, Museo de Arte, São Paulo.

55: *The Temptation of St Anthony*, c.1870, oil on canvas, 54 × 73 cm, Fondation Collection E.G. Bührle, Zurich.

57: *Landscape with a Watermill*, c.1871, oil on canvas, 41 × 54 cm, Yale University Art Gallery, New Haven.

59: *Road at Auvers-sur-Oise*, c.1873–4, oil on canvas, 55.2 × 46.2 cm, National Gallery of Canada, Ottawa.

61: *A Modern Olympia*, 1873, oil on canvas, 46 × 55 cm, Musée d'Orsay, Paris.

63: *Three Bathers*, c.1875–7, oil on canvas, 19 × 22 cm, Musée d'Orsay, Paris.

65: *Plate of Apples*, c.1877, oil on canvas, 46 × 55 cm, Art Institute, Chicago.

67: *Madame Cézanne in a Red Armchair*, c.1877, oil on canvas, 72.5 × 56 cm, Museum of Fine Arts, Boston.

69: *The Bridge at Maincy*, c.1879–80, oil on canvas, 58 × 72 cm, Musée d'Orsay, Paris.

71: *Médan, the Castle,* c.1879–81, oil on canvas, 59 × 72 cm, Museums and Art Galleries, Glasgow.

73: *Self-portrait,* c.1880, oil on canvas, 33 × 26, cm, National Gallery, London.

75: *Apples and Plate of Biscuits,* c.1879–82, oil on canvas, 46 × 55 cm, Musée de l'Orangerie, Paris (Walter Guillaume Collection).

77: *Houses in Provence (Vicinity of L'Estaque),* c.1879–82, oil on canvas, 65 × 81 cm, National Gallery of Art, Washington.

79: *The Sea at L'Estaque,* c.1883, oil on canvas, 73 × 92 cm, Musée du Louvre, Paris (Picasso Bequest).

81: *Still Life with Chest,* c.1882–7, oil on canvas, 71 × 90 cm, Neue Pinakothek, Munich.

83: *View of L'Estaque and the Château d'If,* c.1882–5, oil on canvas, 73 × 60 cm, Fitzwilliam Museum, Cambridge.

85: *House and Farm at the Jas de Bouffan,* c.1885, oil on canvas, 60.5 × 73.5 cm, Narodnie Galerie, Prague.

87: *The Blue Vase,* c.1883–7, oil on canvas, 61 × 50 cm, Musée d'Orsay, Paris

89: *Trees and Houses,* c.1885–8, oil on canvas, 54 × 73 cm, Musée de l'Orangerie, Paris (Walter Guillaume Collection).

91: *Mont Sainte-Victoire,* c.1886–7, oil on canvas, 59.6 × 72.5 cm, The Phillips Collection, Washington.

93: *Mont Sainte-Victoire* c.1885–7, oil on canvas, 54 × 65 cm, Stedelijk Museum, Amsterdam.

95: *Boy in a Red Waistcoat,* 1888–9, oil on canvas, 80 × 64.5 cm, Fondation Collection E.G. Bührle, Zurich.

97: *Madame Cézanne in a Red Dress,* c.1890–4, oil on canvas, 116 × 89 cm, Metropolitan Museum of Art, New York.

99: *Boat and Bathers,* c.1890–4, oil on canvas, 30 × 125 cm, Musée de l'Orangerie, Paris (Walter Guillaume Collection).

101: *Still Life with Peppermint Bottle and Blue Rug,* c.1893–5, oil on canvas, 65 × 81 cm, National Gallery of Art, Washington.

103: *Still Life with Putto,* c.1895, oil on canvas, 71 × 57 cm, Courtauld Institute, London.

105: *The Lake at Annecy,* 1896, oil on canvas, 64 × 81.3, Courtauld Institute, London.

107: *Still Life with Onions* c.1896–8, oil on canvas, 66 × 82 cm, Musée d'Orsay, Paris.

109: *Road to Mas Jolie at the Château-Noir,* 1895–1900, oil on canvas, 79.5 × 64.5 cm, Galerie Beyeler, Basel.

111: *Mont Sainte-Victoire,* c.1897, oil on canvas, 45 × 46 cm, Institute of Arts, Detroit.

113: *Self-portrait with Beret,* c.1898–1900, oil on canvas, 64 × 53.5 cm, Museum of Fine Arts, Boston.

115: *The Millstone in the Park of the Château-Noir,* c.1898–1900, oil on canvas, 73 × 92 cm, Museum of Art, Philadelphia.

117: *The Château-Noir and Mont Sainte-Victoire,* c.1904–6, oil on canvas, 66.1 × 82 cm, Bridgestone Museum, Tokyo.

119: *Portrait of Ambroise Vollard,* 1899, oil on canvas, 100 × 81 cm, Musée du Petit Palais, Paris.

121: *Still Life,* c.1900, oil on canvas, 55 × 46 cm, National Gallery of Art, Washington.

123: *Bathers,* c.1899–1904, oil on canvas, 51.3 × 61.7 cm, Art Institute, Chicago.

125: *Portrait of a Peasant,* c.1900, oil on canvas, 92.7 × 73.7 cm, National Gallery of Canada, Ottawa.

127: *Mont Sainte-Victoire,* c.1903–4, oil on canvas, 83.8 × 65 cm, The Art Museum, Princeton (Henry and Rose Pearlman Foundation).

129: *The Château-Noir,* c.1904, oil on canvas, 74 × 94 cm, Musée Picasso, Paris.

131: *The Large Bathers,* c.1902–6, oil on canvas, 130 × 193 cm, National Gallery, London.

133: *View of Mont Sainte-Victoire from Les Lauves,* c.1902–6, oil on canvas, 63.5 × 83 cm, Kunsthaus, Zurich.

135: *View of Mont Sainte-Victoire from Les Lauves,* c.1904–6, oil on canvas, 60 × 72 cm, Kunstmuseum, Basel.

137: *The Large Bathers,* c.1906, oil on canvas, 208 × 249 cm, Museum of Art, Philadelphia.

139: *Still Life with Pomegranates, Carafe, Sugar Bowl, Bottle and Water Melon* c.1900–06, Watercolour on paper, 30 × 40 cm, Musée du Louvre, Cabinet des Dessins, Paris.